GOLDEN AGE

THE BRILLIANCE OF THE 2018 CHAMPION *Golden State Warriors*

This book is available in quantity at special discounts for your group or organization.
For further information, contact:

Triumph Books LLC
814 North Franklin Street
Chicago, Illinois 60610
Phone: (312) 337-0747
www.triumphbooks.com

Printed in U.S.A.
ISBN: 978-1-62937-560-1

Content packaged by Mojo Media, Inc.
Joe Funk: Editor
Jason Hinman: Creative Director

All interior photos by AP Images

Front and Back Cover Photos: USA TODAY Sports Images

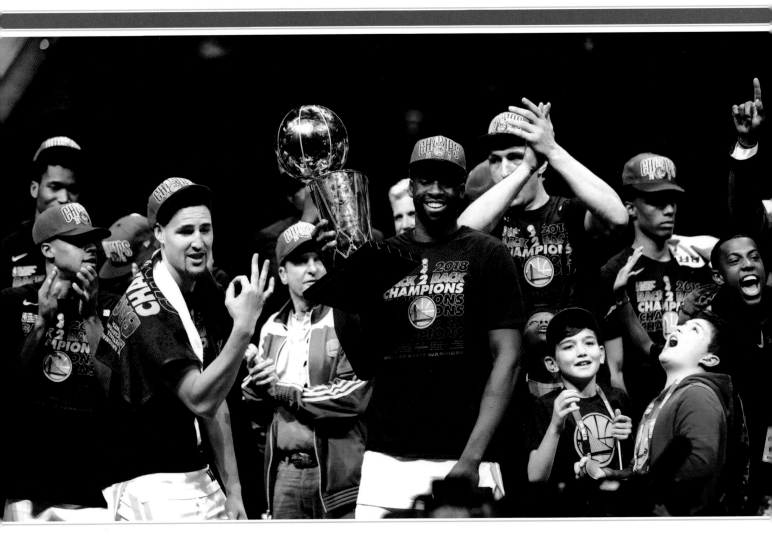

CONTENTS

INTRODUCTION

"IF YOU LOOK UP THERE, THAT IS A VERY LONELY FLAG. WE WANT ANOTHER ONE!"

—Joe Lacob, November 15th, 2010

When Warriors co-owner Joe Lacob said this shortly after buying the team with Peter Guber in 2010, it felt like an impossibility. For more than 30 years, the Warriors had been one of the most forgettable teams in the NBA. For the Warriors and their fans, a Slam Dunk Contest victory by one of their players or a playoff appearance was a cause for great celebration. Scoring an upset over an opponent in the playoffs was a once-in-a-lifetime accomplishment to be celebrated and cherished.

But while it initially seemed like hubris or delusion, Lacob's dreams of more championship banners hanging in the rafters for the Warriors became a reality.

On Friday, June 8th, The Warriors completed their sweep of the Cleveland Cavaliers, defeating them 108–85 in Game 4 to claim the 2018 NBA championship. For the Warriors, this was their third title in four years and was another highlight in one of the most dominant stretches in NBA history.

Through a series of smart drafts (picking Klay Thompson, Harrison Barnes, and Draymond Green to join Stephen Curry), trades (sending Monta Ellis to Milwaukee in exchange for Andrew Bogut), and free agent signings (bringing in Andre Iguodala, Shaun Livingston, and, most prominently, Kevin Durant), Lacob, Guber, GM Bob Myers, and head coach Steve Kerr have transformed an irrelevant franchise into the class of the league.

The road to the 2018 title was much rockier than the one these Warriors had trod in previous seasons.

There was the wear-and-tear that came along with playing in three consecutive NBA Finals, along with the knowledge that their season would be judged based upon what they did in the postseason and not in the regular season. Their focus would wax and wane, their play during stretches of the regular season could be less-than-perfect.

The Warriors also dealt with a rash of injuries in 2018, including losing Curry to a Grade 2 MCL Sprain for the final 10 games of the regular season and the first round of the playoffs.

The Warriors also had to face much tougher competition on their way to the title. Most notable was a Houston Rockets team that added Chris Paul and P.J. Tucker to go with James Harden, Trevor Ariza, and Clint Capela, that pushed the Warriors to seven games in the Western Conference Finals.

In the regular season the Warriors also had to contend with an Oklahoma City Thunder team that added Paul George and Carmelo Anthony to play alongside the 2017 MVP Russell Westbrook. There were also tougher foes in the Eastern Conference, with Kyrie Irving joining the young core of Jaylen Brown and Jayson Tatum in Boston.

And, lest we forget, there was the great LeBron James and his Cleveland Cavaliers waiting in the NBA Finals for a fourth-straight season.

But in spite of all these obstacles and challenges, the Warriors still managed to persevere. While this season was not as easy as the previous three, with

Owner Joe Lacob cradles the third championship trophy for the Warriors in four years, a dream realized for him and fellow owner Peter Guber.

the team at times not looking like the presumptive champion everyone assumed them to be, in the biggest moments they displayed the will to win and the poise to overcome any challenge. The ride might have been a bit choppier, a bit bumpier, than in the past, but with those obstacles along the way the Warriors harnessed the toughness and determination that defines their greatness.

With this 2018 championship, the Warriors join the pantheon of great modern NBA dynasties—the Showtime Lakers, Larry Bird's Celtics, Michael Jordan's Bulls, the Duncan-Popovich Spurs, the LeBron-Wade Heat teams. The Warriors also solidified their place amongst the great teams in Bay Area professional sports history, earning a place alongside the Swingin' A's of the 1970s, John Madden's Raiders teams, the Bill Walsh-Joe Montana San Francisco 49ers, and the San Francisco Giants of the early 2010s.

We are currently watching one of the greatest periods in the history of professional basketball and the team that is leading the way in this new golden age are the Golden State Warriors, the 2018 NBA champions. ■

NBA FINALS, GAME 1

MAY 31, 2018 | OAKLAND, CALIFORNIA
WARRIORS 124, CAVALIERS 114 OT

WORKING OVERTIME

Warriors Survive LeBron's 51 points in Epic Game 1

In one of the strangest and yet most exciting NBA Finals games in recent memory, the Golden State Warriors took Game 1 from the Cleveland Cavaliers in overtime 124–114.

It was an exciting game, one that featured 15 lead changes and 17 ties. But in the pivotal moments where the game hung in the balance, the Warriors were able to capitalize on their opportunities as they took a 1–0 lead in the 2018 NBA Finals.

After addressing questions about why he hadn't yet won a Finals MVP, Stephen Curry came out in Thursday night's game and played like someone who was looking to win one. Curry scored 29 points in the Game 1 victory, while also handing out nine assists and grabbing six rebounds.

Curry did much of his damage from beyond the arc, going 5-for-11 from three-point range. One of those made three-pointers came seconds before halftime, and he knocked it down from 38 feet just before the buzzer sounded to tie things up at 56 after one half of play.

Curry's offensive impact was vital for the Warriors in the second half. With Kevin Durant struggling, Curry became the best offensive option for the Warriors, and the Warriors turned to him to get the win.

With under a minute to go and the Warriors trailing, Curry got three points the old-fashioned way, making the circus-style driving layup and then adding the free throw to give the Warriors a brief one-point lead. Though that lead wouldn't last as it would take overtime to determine the winner of this game, Curry worked hard to get his team the victory.

While Curry played exceedingly well and led his team to the win, LeBron James put in one of the greatest individual performances in NBA Finals history in Game 1. James scored 51 points in Game 1, the fifth-highest point total in NBA Finals history (and the most in a loss).

The Warriors had no answer for James, who could drive to the basket at will while also making plenty of shots from three-point range. Even if Andre Iguodala had been able to play, the Warriors still might not have been able to slow him down.

"It's tough to stop him," Durant said after the game. "Especially, he's getting a lot of screens, he's getting Steph on him a lot [in switches], and that's what the mismatch is, getting the bigs on him."

The Warriors are going up against one of the greatest players in the history of the game in LeBron James during these Finals. He is a very tough man to deal with, even if the Warriors play better defense. In Game 1 James reminded everyone watching that a dominant performance from him can be enough to (nearly) get a victory.

One scary moment for the Warriors came early in this game as Klay Thompson and J.R. Smith chased down a loose ball. Smith slipped and fell into the back of Thompson's legs, causing the Warriors' All-Star guard to twist his left leg very hard before falling down. In visible pain and limping, Thompson went back into the Warriors locker room, and many thought his Finals might be over.

However, Thompson returned to the Warriors' bench and re-entered the lineup in the second quarter. What looked like a very nasty injury was ruled a left

LeBron James, who scored 51 points, goes in for a layup during Game 1 of the NBA Finals.

lateral leg contusion, and he was able to return to action. Thompson scored 22 points in the rest of Thursday night's game, going 5-for-8 from three-point range.

After the game head coach Steve Kerr said that Thompson "took a 35-footer on his first possession back on the floor. So we knew he was okay."

It will get lost in the shuffle with James' remarkable performance and the exciting way the game ended, but Thompson quietly played in a very gutsy and important game that allowed the Warriors to get the win.

Even before the closing seconds, this first game of the 2018 NBA Finals was already very exciting. Every time one team seemed to have an advantage, the other one battled back and tied things up as the game went back and forth.

With the Cavaliers up two in those closing seconds, the Warriors got the ball to Durant who drove into the lane to try and tie the game. Durant drew contact from both Jeff Green and James.

Initially, the referees called a very dubious offensive foul on Durant. However, after consulting with replay to see if James was in the restricted area, the officials saw enough evidence to overturn the call and change it to a blocking foul on James and give Durant two free throws, which he made to tie the game.

It was a very important moment in the game, but ultimately the correct call to make as James was not set when he came into contact with Durant and he was turned slightly.

With the Cavaliers trailing by one point with less than 20 seconds left to go, George Hill drew a foul on Thompson and went to the free-throw line. Hill, who joined the Cavaliers as a result of their many trade deadline deals, made the first free throw. However, Hill missed the second, and Smith secured the rebound for the Cavaliers.

Rather than going up for a shot, Smith dribbled the ball out of the paint and to the perimeter, allowing time to expire before the Cavaliers could get a shot up, thus allowing the game to reach overtime.

What appeared to happen was that Smith thought the Cavaliers had the lead and that he should run out the clock. This was what Smith seemed to indicate to James

Kevin Durant, who had 26 points and nine rebounds, shoots over Kevin Love during Game 1 of the NBA Finals.

and the rest of his teammates in the moment and was confirmed by Cavaliers head coach Tyronn Lue.

However, in his postgame comments, Smith offered a different explanation. He said: "I was trying to get enough to bring it out to get a shot off. I knew we were tied, I thought we were going to call timeout. If I thought we were ahead, I'd have held onto the ball and let them foul me."

Whatever the reason, the combination of Hill missing that second free throw and Smith not doing the smart thing after securing that rebound cost the Cavaliers a victory. The Warriors were more than happy to take that opening and steal a game they'd probably thought they had let slip away.

In the overtime period, the Warriors dominated the Cavaliers 17–7 to earn the 10-point victory in Game 1. But in the closing seconds of the game and with the outcome all but decided, there was some extra drama.

Shaun Livingston took a shot with the 24-second clock about to expire and a few seconds left on the game clock. Cavaliers forward Tristan Thompson took issue with Livingston trying to score more points (as opposed to taking a turnover, something that Warriors head coach Steve Kerr constantly preaches against). Thompson fouled Livingston hard on the play—so hard that he earned a flagrant-2 foul that ejected him from the game.

As he was leaving the court, Thompson got into a back-and-forth with Draymond Green. Eventually, Thompson pushed the ball into Green's face and shoved the Warriors forward.

Green responded (though he didn't throw a punch or strike Thompson at all), and there was much posturing and trash talking from both teams. Thompson was finally forced from the court. Because he did not exit in a timely manner after his initial ejection, Thompson could potentially be suspended for Game 2, stretching an already thin Cavaliers team even thinner.

But this provided an emotional and exciting end to an exciting first game of the 2018 NBA Finals. For a matchup many professed to be sick of and a series many worried would be boring and stale, Game 1 was anything but that and gave everyone plenty of reason to be excited about what was to come. ∎

Klay Thompson and Draymond Green envelop LeBron James, but nothing could really slow the Cavaliers' star.

JUNE 3, 2018 | OAKLAND, CALIFORNIA
WARRIORS 122, CAVALIERS 103

ON CLOUD NINE

Curry Sets Three-Point Record During Fourth-Quarter Outburst

After their thrilling overtime win in Game 1, the Golden State Warriors led from wire-to-wire in Game 2, handing the Cleveland Cavaliers a 122–103 defeat. With the win, the Warriors took a 2–0 series lead in these 2018 NBA Finals.

Leading the way for the Warriors was Stephen Curry, who played like someone who is going after a Finals MVP award. Curry scored 33 points in the Warriors' Game 2 win while also contributing eight assists and grabbing seven rebounds. Curry set a record for three-pointers in a NBA Finals game with his nine makes in Game 2, passing Ray Allen and his eight made three-pointers for the Boston Celtics in 2010.

After the game, Curry downplayed the achievement while focusing on the team's success in getting the victory.

"I never woke up and was like, all right, let's go get nine threes and get the record," Curry said. "It was more so about playing the game the right way, having good intentions out there on the court, and good things happen."

Part of what made that three-point barrage possible was the ability of Curry (and the other Warriors players) to get into the lane and score in the paint, especially early in the game. The Warriors scored 50 points in the paint, shooting 25-of-35 in that area. The Warriors also shot 69.5 percent on two-point shots, taking advantage of a Cavaliers defensive gameplan that was much more focused on stopping three-pointers.

Because the Warriors were able to get free in the paint, the Cavaliers defense could not stay out at the three-point line. Once they had to make that adjustment, it freed Curry up and allowed him to get hot from long distance.

The bulk of Curry's three-point assault came in the fourth quarter. Though the Warriors led the entire game, the Cavaliers cut into the Warriors' lead throughout the first and second half, taking a double-digit deficit. Every time it seemed like the Warriors were ready to pull away, the Cavaliers had an answer to keep things close. But in the fourth quarter, Curry erupted and went 5-for-5 from three-point range to seal the Warriors victory and turn the last three-and-a-half minutes of the game into garbage time.

"Nine threes and seemed to hit the big shot every time we needed one," Warriors head coach Steve Kerr said.

Part of why the Warriors were able to score like that in the paint had to do with Kerr's decision to start JaVale McGee at center. After playing some very strong minutes in the Warriors' Game 1 win, Kerr elected to play McGee from the very beginning. McGee responded by scoring 12 points in Game 2, going 6-of-6 from the field, and giving the Warriors energy and defense.

Although their defense looked lackluster at times during Game 1, the Warriors did a much better job guarding the Cavaliers in Game 2. After scoring 51 points in Game 1, LeBron James ended with 29 points in Game 2, along with 13 assists and 9 rebounds. Outside of James and Kevin Love, who scored 22 points, no other Cavaliers player was able to get going on offense.

With Andre Iguodala still sidelined, both Kevin Durant and Draymond Green took on the challenge of

Stephen Curry, who nailed nine three-pointers (an NBA Finals record) during Game 2, celebrates after scoring.

guarding James. Though James was still able to score and be an offensive force, the Warriors forwards did a good job of keeping the Cavaliers' star from having a similar game to the one he had in Game 1.

That was just one facet of a much better game for Durant, who scored 26 points on 10-of-14 shooting to go with his nine rebounds and seven assists. In Game 2 Durant was much more focused—whether on offense or guarding James on defense. After struggling at times in the Western Conference Finals against the Houston Rockets and in Game 1 of the NBA Finals against the Cavaliers, Durant came back with an impressive performance in Game 2 that effectively complimented Curry's record-setting game.

Though his status remained in doubt until just before tip-off, Klay Thompson played in Game 2 after suffering a scary looking left lateral leg contusion in Game 1. Thompson scored 20 points while also contributing good defense. After walking with a noticeable limp at Saturday's media session, Thompson's play on the court was impressive.

"The ankle feels great," Thompson said. "I won't do much tomorrow and I'll do a little bit Tuesday. But I'm just going to conserve all I've got for Wednesday because I don't want to play with it."

The Warriors also got some help from their bench, including 10 points from Shaun Livingston and a big three-pointer at the end of the third quarter from David West that provided the Warriors with a cushion as the game moved into the fourth quarter.

For the third straight year, the Warriors will head to Cleveland with a 2–0 lead in the NBA Finals. But they know that having that lead guarantees nothing and that they'll need to be at their best come game time on Wednesday.

"It will be very important for us to be locked in from the jump on the defensive side of the ball and not giving those guys easy shots," Green said. "They've got a great crowd and they really feed off it." ■

Defense by Draymond Green and Stephen Curry helped limit LeBron James and the Cavaliers to 41.1 percent shooting in Game 2.

With Andre Iguodala sidelined, Draymond Green serves as one of the main defenders against LeBron James in Game 2.

NBA FINALS, GAME 3

JUNE 6, 2018 | CLEVELAND, OHIO
WARRIORS 110, CAVALIERS 102

DURANT DOMINATES

KD Scores a Playoff Career-High 43 points in Comeback Victory

In the confines of the Quicken Loans Arena in Cleveland, the Warriors won an exciting Game 3 of the NBA Finals that came down to the final minutes. They came from behind to defeat the Cavaliers 110–102 after trailing for the entire first half. The win gave the Warriors a 3–0 lead in the 2018 NBA Finals, which they could end with a victory in Game 4 on Friday night.

In a hostile environment and with his team struggling to match up against one of the greatest players in the history of the NBA, Kevin Durant played perhaps the greatest game of his career. Durant scored a career playoff-high 43 points on 15-of-23 shooting, including 6-of-9 from three-point range.

In the first half, one in which the Warriors never led while the Cavaliers led by as many as 13 points, Durant scored 24 points while the rest of the Warriors' roster scored just 28.

Three of Durant's 24 first-half points came on a three-point shot in the closing seconds of the second quarter that cut the Cavaliers' lead to just six points.

There was no drop-off for Durant in the second half as he continued his assault on the basket, scoring 19 points over the third and fourth quarters.

Durant's ability to go out and get his shot was extremely important for the Warriors as they went back and forth with the Cavaliers, getting the lead and then watching them take it back. In the second half, there were 11 lead changes, and the game was tied eight times.

Thus Durant's ability to allow the Warriors to keep pace and prevent the Cavaliers from growing any lead was vital.

With the Warriors up by just three points and around a minute left to go in the game, Durant made the killing stroke, the coup de grace.

Pulling up from 33 feet from the basketball hoop, Durant smoothly drilled the jumper that gave the Warriors the 106–100 lead and served as the exclamation point on the Warriors forward's masterful performance.

Durant's shot came from roughly the same spot where he took the three-pointer that won Game 3 for the Warriors in the 2017 NBA Finals. But it wasn't quite the same spot.

"No, that wasn't the same shot," James said. "The one he made tonight was about four or five feet behind the one he made last year."

Durant's excellence was not limited to scoring as he finished the game with 13 rebounds, doing a much better job of boxing out and battling for the ball. Even though Durant was an unstoppable offensive force and things seemed to flow through him in Game 3, he still had seven assists and did not become too locked into an isolation-heavy approach.

"It just happened within the flow," Durant said. "I wasn't expecting to come out or shoot a lot of shots or look to score. I was just trying to play great defense and run the plays that Coach draws up and just run with the flow of what our offense is like throughout the game."

It was an amazing performance by Durant and one he gave on the biggest stage in the toughest environment when his team needed it the most.

The Warriors needed every one of Durant's points because their other MVP, Stephen Curry, struggled in

In addition to his incredible offensive performance, Kevin Durant's great defense, including this block on LeBron James, led the Warriors to the Game 3 win.

Game 3. One game after setting the record for most made three-pointers in a Finals game, Curry was 1-of-10 from three-point range, 3-of-16 overall, and scored just 11 points.

Curry's rough night came about for a number of reasons. Some of it was sheer bad luck; even the greatest shooters can have games where the ball bounces the wrong way. Curry did get some open looks. He just missed the shots.

The Cavaliers' defense played a role in Curry's underwhelming performance. They did a better job staying with him and contesting. The Cavaliers defended one play—when Curry passes it to someone in the paint and then sprints to the corner to get the return pass and put up a three-pointer—much better.

Finally, the Cavaliers' offense also might have played a role in Curry's poor shooting numbers. It was clear that the Cavaliers, and LeBron James in particular, were making a point of directing their offense at Curry and making him have to work on the defensive end.

At some point, all that extra battling and struggling is going to catch up with you. It might have with Curry in Game 3, sapping him of some of his energy and thus making it difficult to get his shots off in the way he wants.

For all his struggles, Curry did end Game 3 with six assists and went on a personal 5–0 run to turn a one-point Cavaliers lead into a four-point Warriors lead with just more than two minutes remaining. Part of that run was Curry's first three-point make that Durant described as "the biggest shot" of the game.

"It was a crazy night all the way around," Curry said. "[I] tried to still play with energy and tried to do the little things here and there to help the team, but to get one, one good shot down the stretch and still have confidence in myself to knock it down. My teammates were talking to me the whole game, which was helpful. Thankfully, that last one went in."

Not surprisingly, the Cavaliers played much better at home than they did in the first two games of these NBA Finals at Oracle Arena. James was outstanding once again, posting a triple-double with 33 points, 11 assists, and 10 rebounds. The Cavaliers also got 20 points and 13 rebounds from Kevin Love while Rodney Hood came off the bench and scored 15 points of his own.

The Cavaliers also did a good job pulling in offensive rebounds as they ended the game with 15, 10 of which came in the first half. The ability to get second opportunities at offensive possessions (the Cavaliers took 11 more field-goal attempts than the Warriors did) allowed them to get that first-half lead and keep up with Durant's dominant performance.

In the first half, the Cavaliers shot 49.1 percent from the field and 42.9 percent from three-point range. However, in the second half, those percentages would dip a great deal as they shot 35.9 percent from the field and 17.6 percent from three-point range. James was the only player the Cavaliers could count on in the second half, which was not enough to get them the Game 3 win.

After missing the previous six games, Andre Iguodala returned to the Warriors' lineup in Game 3. In his return to action, the 2015 Finals MVP played nearly 22 minutes and scored eight points and was a plus-14.

"He's at plus-14, typical Andre line," head coach Steve Kerr said. "You might look at it and go, yeah, he had eight points and whatever. But he gives us another guy to guard LeBron and he gives us another guy to settle us down and keep us on the right path."

Though he was clearly not at 100 percent, Iguodala worked hard when he was switched onto James and made him work for his field goals. With Durant on the team, the duty of defending James does not fall solely on Iguodala, but the veteran is a particularly adept defender who makes James' job difficult on offense.

Though he still looked hobbled at times and was seen walking with a limp after the game, Iguodala still threw down a vicious dunk with under two minutes to go that pushed a one-point Warriors lead to three.

In a game like this one, an important one being played before an angry and raucous crowd, it was very helpful to have the savvy presence of Iguodala on the court to make sure everything was running smoothly. ■

Kevin Durant, who went 15-of-23 from the field in Game 3, guides his team during the Warriors' comeback victory.

JUNE 8, 2018 | CLEVELAND, OHIO
WARRIORS 108, CAVALIERS 85

THREE-SWEEP!

Warriors Capture Third Title in Four Years in Dominating Fashion

The Golden State Warriors claimed the 2018 NBA Finals with a definitive Game 4 victory over the Cleveland Cavaliers, winning 108–85 at Quicken Loans Arena to complete the sweep.

After playing sub-par in Game 3, Stephen Curry came out and put on an incredible performance in Game 4. Curry scored 37 points in the Warriors blowout win, including going 7-for-15 from three-point range. After scoring just 11 points in Game 3, Curry surpassed that total in the first quarter, scoring 12 points to start out the game. Curry scored 20 points in the first half of Game 4, tying his highest point total in one half in his 22 NBA Finals games.

Curry's influence on Game 4 was not limited to his offensive outburst, finishing the game with six rebounds, three steals, and three blocks. Curry's defense, much like it was in Game 3, was strong if slightly underappreciated.

In these Finals, Curry averaged 27.5 points per game along with six rebounds and 6.8 assists. While Curry did not win the Finals MVP, he certainly played like one and was more than deserving of one with the performance he gave.

Warriors head coach Steve Kerr addressed this postgame, about Curry's lack of concern over these individual accolades. "It's not like there was a transformation. Steph's always been one of the most unselfish people you can be around. He's really an amazing human being," Kerr said after the Game 4 win. "It's rare that you see this combination, and I've said this

before, but it's worth saying again, the combination of incredible talent and humility, that is such a powerful force in our locker room. In many ways it sets the tone for the whole organization."

While Curry's offensive performance was dazzling, Kevin Durant's all-around performance was the other key component to the Warriors' series-clinching victory. In this closeout game, Durant posted a triple double on his way to winning Finals MVP. Durant's performance in Games 3 and 4 was nothing short of amazing, as he played extremely well in front of a hostile and vocal Cleveland crowd.

Looking back on the past two seasons and some of the criticism that has been directed at him, Durant said this postgame: "I know what I bring to the game. I know how I approach the game, how hard I work, how much I care. I think that's the stuff I try to focus on more than anything is just being a professional basketball player and doing stuff for me and the team. So I pride myself on that and everything else is just noise." In Game 4, it was clear how much work and effort Durant puts into his game. It was on full display and it was part of why he won his second-straight Finals MVP.

In some ways, Game 4 was a perfect encapsulation of the Warriors' season. Stellar play by Curry and Durant, and an impressive third quarter. As they have all season, the Warriors dominated the third quarter, 25-13. Klay Thompson was the hot hand for the Warriors in the third. Thompson scored just 10 points in the game but

LeBron James is called for a charging foul against Stephen Curry during Game 4. The Warriors frustrated LeBron into five fouls and six turnovers in the game.

all 10 came in the third quarter as the Warriors pushed their lead to 21 points, turning the fourth quarter into extended garbage time.

The Warriors' impressive ball movement was on full display in Game 4 as well. The Warriors had 25 assists in Game 4, led by Durant's 10 and Draymond Green's nine. The Warriors used this ball movement to attack a porous Cavaliers defense, one that was susceptible to back cuts and did not do well defending the Warriors' transition offense.

Returning in Game 3 after missing six games, Andre Iguodala turned in an outstanding performance in Game 4, one reminiscent of his 2015 NBA Finals when he won the Finals MVP. Iguodala scored 11 points while going 3-for-6 from three-point range. Iguodala played outstanding defense as well, as he picked up two steals and one block while having to deal with LeBron James on numerous possessions.

In his postgame comments, Kerr brought this up, saying "I thought one of the keys to the series, to be honest, was Andre returning in Game 3. It gave the rest of the guys some relief, Draymond, K.D., Klay, so

Opposite: Steph Curry shoots around LeBron James. Curry had another terrific game, with 37 points and seven three-pointers. Above: Draymond Green is defended by Kevin Love. Green distributed the ball well in the game, finishing with nine assists.

we were able to put Andre on LeBron, and that gave everybody else some rest. It allowed us to change the look. Andre's one of the best defenders in the league, and he did a fantastic job in Games 3 and 4."

James still managed to score 23 points in Game 4 to go with his eight assists and seven rebounds, but he wasn't able to get rolling against a tough Warriors defense. The Warriors did a good job of locking down the Cavaliers' supporting cast. Kevin Love scored 13 points and J.R. Smith and Rodney Hood each scored 10, but it was clear that the Cavaliers couldn't get anything going against a Warriors defense that held the Cavaliers to 34.5% from the field and 29.6% from three-point range.

The Warriors played one of their best games of the season in Game 4. They were tough on defense, had great performances from their two former MVPs, moved the ball, and blew a team out in the third quarter to render the game a fait accompli even before the fourth quarter began. With that dominating performance, the Warriors swept away the Cavaliers in the 2018 Finals, winning their third title in four years and cementing their place amongst the greatest teams in the history of the NBA. ∎

Above: Fans who packed Oracle Arena in Oakland to watch Game 4 from afar had plenty to cheer about, celebrating another championship for their Warriors. Opposite: Jordan Bell (2) and Draymond Green (23) celebrate clinching the 2018 title at the end of Game 4.

TAKE TWO

Kevin Durant Claims Second Consecutive Finals MVP

Kevin Durant claimed his second-straight NBA Finals MVP award, closing out the 2018 NBA Finals with two dominant performances on the road at Quicken Loans Arena in Cleveland.

After the first two games of the Finals, Durant winning this award did not seem terribly likely. Durant struggled in Game 1, scoring 26 points but needing 22 shots to do so. Durant also struggled defensively and with his rebounding, frequently getting boxed out and allowing the Cavaliers to secure offensive rebounds leading to additional scoring opportunities.

Durant's performance in Game 2 was much better, though it was overshadowed by Stephen Curry's NBA Finals-record nine three-pointers. In Game 2, Durant scored 26 points, doing so much more efficiently as he only needed 14 shots to reach that total. Durant's defense, especially on LeBron James, was much better in Game 2, as was his rebounding intensity.

But the case for Durant's MVP was made largely from his performances in Games 3 and 4.

Durant's Game 3 was one for the ages. With both Curry and Klay Thompson struggling, Durant took the Warriors on his back and willed them to the win. Durant scored 43 points in the game, including a three-pointer from 33 feet out that was the dagger. In that Game 3, Durant also had 13 rebounds and seven assists. But it was Durant's scoring, picking up his struggling teammates and giving the Warriors the 3-0 series lead, that Warriors fans will remember for years to come.

Durant did not to do as much scoring in the closeout Game 4, as he contributed just 20 points. However, Durant had 12 rebounds and 10 assists, putting up a triple-double in a closeout game on the road. Durant's defense was great once again in Game 4, as he protected the rim and had three blocks.

What was most impressive, and what perhaps gave him the edge in Finals MVP-voting over Curry (who also had an MVP-worthy series) was that Durant gave these performances on the road. Durant stepped up his game in a hostile environment, especially in Game 3 when his teammates were not playing well.

In the 2018 Finals, Durant averaged 28.8 points per game along with 10.8 rebounds, 7.8 assists, and two blocks per game.

In these Finals, Durant showed that he is not just a great scorer but a great basketball player, affecting all facets of the game.

On the brightest and biggest of stages, Durant showed exactly why he is a perfect fit for this Warriors team and why to achieve their loftiest goals, they needed him to be a part of this organization. ■

Kevin Durant holds the NBA championship and MVP trophies after the Warriors clinched the title over the Cavs. Durant has had a picturesque two years with Golden State, winning two championships and two NBA Finals MVP awards.

REGULAR SEASON

Stephen Curry and Draymond Green enjoy the ceremony honoring their 2016–17 championship, which took place prior to the first game of the 2017–18 regular season.

Head Coach

STEVE KERR

Kerr Thinks Outside the Box, Doesn't Stick to Sports

For Steve Kerr the 2017–18 season was perhaps the most challenging one of his tenure as Warriors head coach. Some of those challenges came from off-the court issues.

As opposed to previous seasons, when the Warriors head coach was battling persistent pain due to complications after back surgery, this year's off-court troubles came from another source—the world of politics and current events.

Continuing where he left off last season, Kerr again served as a thoughtful voice on the social and political issues of our time. Kerr has been particularly vocal concerning the prevalence of acts of gun violence, incidents of which have been occurring at a seemingly higher rate in the past year.

Kerr has been extremely critical of the Trump administration and Republican-led Congress' unwillingness to deal with the recurrence of these incidents through stronger legislation.

"Hopefully we'll find enough people, first of all, to vote good people in, but hopefully we can find enough people with courage to help our citizens remain safe and focus on the real safety issues," Kerr said in the aftermath of the school shooting in Parkland, Florida, "not building some stupid wall for billions of dollars that has nothing to do with our safety, but actually protecting us from what truly is dangerous, which is maniacs with semiautomatic weapons just slaughtering our children. It's disgusting."

Kerr, whose father Malcolm was killed by gun violence during a terrorist attack in Lebanon, is one who believes that everyone should be involved and care about what is going on in the world, even athletes and coaches.

"When people say stick to sports, stick to coaching, whatever—that means nothing," Kerr said. "We all have a voice."

One way in which Kerr made use of his voice and the platform afforded to him as the coach of one of the best teams in sports came in March of 2018. Along with congressman Ro Khanna and student activists from Parkland, the Warriors head coach organized a town hall at Newark High School that elicited a robust and thoughtful discussion of these incidents of gun violence and what can be done to curtail them.

While Kerr was serving as an example of what a thoughtful and engaged citizen looks like off the court during the 2017–18 season, he also played the part of the successful head coach on the sidelines as well.

This season presented numerous new challenges for Kerr, namely having to coach a veteran team with championship-or-bust expectations. Knowing that what

Steve Kerr, who learned under Phil Jackson and Gregg Popovich, gives instruction during Game 2 of the 2018 NBA Finals.

really mattered was what they did in the postseason, the Warriors did not seem as overly concerned with their play in the regular season as they had in the past. Kerr himself acknowledged this.

"You feel it after a number of years. The team has a different vibe around it, and you've gotta fight through that," the Warriors head coach said early in the season. "When I got here three years ago, these guys were bouncing off the walls every night…They had this hunger, this motivation."

This season that diminishment of the regular-season hunger and knowing that being ready for the postseason was the most important thing kept the Warriors from being engaged all the time.

Throughout the season Kerr sought different ways to keep his players engaged and focused while keeping the larger, championship picture in mind. One unique and effective way Kerr found to keep his players engaged was on display in the team's February 12th game against the Phoenix Suns.

Throughout that 129–83 Warriors victory, Andre Iguodala, David West, and the sidelined Draymond Green all took turns drawing up plays in the huddle. The positive effect was immediately grasped as the team looked extremely excited and engaged while playing a lottery-bound Suns team that they might have been tempted to otherwise overlook.

After the game, Kerr was asked about this decision and explained his rationale.

"As coaches, our job is to nudge them in the right direction, guide them, but we don't control them," he said. "They determine their own fate. And I don't feel like we've focused well at all over the last month, and it just seemed like the right thing to do. And they communicated really well together and they drew up some nice plays."

It was a bright decision made by Kerr to cede control of this game to the players, one that not too many coaches in the NBA would be willing to do. Recognizing that a change in the in-game voice might be

Always cool and collected, Steve Kerr arrives for a game against the Miami Heat in December of 2017.

good for the team was definitely another manifestation of the humble, self-aware nature possessed by the Warriors' head coach.

"I have not reached them for the last month," Kerr said. "They're tired of my voice. I'm tired of my voice. It's been a long haul these last few years, and I wasn't reaching them, and we just figured it was probably a good night to pull a trick out of the hat and do something different."

Kerr's move was akin to the teacher whose students aren't doing the work or paying attention (which often happens if a break or vacation is coming up). The teacher makes the students do the work and, essentially, teach the class as a way of making them actually focus and engage with the material. This is what happened with the Warriors. The team looked more engaged and focused than it had in quite a while.

Kerr even acknowledged the scholarly quality to this move by saying that to his players he probably "sounds like Charlie Brown's teacher or parent or whoever's voice that is. At this point, that's what I sound like to them."

Some saw this as a sign of disrespect toward the Suns—that the Warriors thought so little of their opponent that they just let the players coach for the hell of it. Rather than being a sign of disrespect, however, this was a very forward-thinking decision made by Kerr to get the team out of its habit of lackadaisical play.

"I liked the move personally," Suns guard Devin Booker said. "If I was a coach, I'd do that throughout the year, so I wouldn't even look at it as disrespectful."

Whether being an increasingly important voice on social issues for finding ways to motivate an extremely talented yet often disengaged team, it was a season of countless challenges for Steve Kerr. However, while there were numerous problems to overcome, the reward at the end of it all—another NBA championship—must have made it all worthwhile. ∎

Steve Kerr speaks to Newark Memorial High School in California during a town hall-style discussion about gun violence.

A LONG GRIND

Between Injuries and Bouts of Apathy, the Regular Season Wasn't Easy

The Warriors' 2017–18 regular season was perhaps the most vexing of their recent championship run. Steve Kerr addressed it in the preseason.

"Three years in a row in the Finals, trying to make it a fourth. Very few teams in the history of the league have done that, and there's a reason," Kerr said. "It's a long haul, so we're going to have to navigate the season, pace ourselves but not lose our edge, and that's the balance we're looking for."

Whether it was the wear and tear of the previous three seasons or the knowledge that their decision would be judged as a success or a failure based solely on what they do in the playoffs, the Warriors did not start out the regular season as crisply as they could have. The Warriors lost three of their first seven games, including two at Oracle Arena, and suffered a 17-point blowout loss at Oklahoma City to Russell Westbrook and the Oklahoma City Thunder just before Thanksgiving.

After that blowout loss in Oklahoma City, Kevin Durant made it clear that the issue is the Warriors not playing as well as they could.

"The story's about the game," Durant said. "We lost. They kicked our ass. They played a great game. You should give them credit for how they played, and we should be better."

Turnovers were largely the cause of this somewhat uneven start and the biggest example of how the Warriors' on-court play was not matching up with their championship aspirations. The Warriors gave the ball away 25 times in a home loss to the Detroit Pistons on October 30 and averaged close to 16 turnovers-per-game in the month of November, including a 22-turnover game in that blowout November loss to the Thunder.

HITTING THEIR STRIDE

As the calendar turned from November to December, the Warriors' play picked up. At the beginning of the month, however, it looked like the Warriors' struggles would continue as Stephen Curry suffered an ankle sprain on December 4 that would keep him out for multiple weeks.

But even with the absence of their two-time MVP, the Warriors still had an impressive stretch going before Curry came back. Part of why the Warriors were able to do this was because of their defensive intensity led by Durant, Draymond Green, and Andre Iguodala.

The Warriors' ability to win with defense when Curry was sidelined was on display during their Christmas win against the Cleveland Cavaliers. In that game the Warriors held LeBron James to just 20 points and the Cavaliers to 31.8 percent from the field.

During the month of December, a month in which Curry played just two games, the Warriors were winning games with defense. In December they held opponents to a season-low 102.7 points per game while holding

Stephen Curry slices between Pelicans defenders during the Warriors' second game of the year, a victory in which Curry had 28 points.

opponents to 42.4 percent from the field. With Curry out of the lineup, the Warriors turned to Durant as the chief offensive weapon, and he responded by averaging 27 points, 7.1 rebounds, and 5.9 assists per game in the month of December.

When Curry returned to the lineup on December 30 against the Memphis Grizzlies, the Warriors continued their refocused play well into January and February up until the All-Star break. During that stretch the Warriors went 15–6 and played some of their best basketball of the regular season. To be certain there were some letdowns along the way, including a 20-point loss to the Thunder in Oakland, in which the Warriors turned the ball over 25 times.

But that stretch of the Warriors' season included a win against the Houston Rockets in which Curry, Klay Thompson, and Green all combined for 74 of the Warriors' 124 points. The Warriors traveled to Cleveland to play the Cavaliers on January 15. In this NBA Finals preview, the Warriors won 118–108 behind Durant's 32 points, eight assists, and five rebounds, along with Curry's 23 points while going 4-of-8 from long distance. The win was the Warriors' seventh win against the Cavaliers in the last nine meetings and was their third consecutive road win against Eastern Conference playoff teams (beating the Milwaukee Bucks and Toronto Raptors before defeating the Cavaliers).

The Warriors also won a 109–105 game at Oracle Arena against the Boston Celtics, avenging an early-season loss to the Eastern Conference squad. The game became a showdown between the Boston Celtics' Kyrie Irving (who scored 37 points) and Curry (who scored a season-high 49 points).

"We try to bring the best out of each other," Curry said. "Tonight was one of those nights, just a fun way to play."

It was Curry's best performance of the 2017–18 season. He took over the game and ignited the Oracle crowd with his display of spectacular shooting. Curry had his best stretch of basketball in the month of January, scoring 29.5 points per game and recording 6.7

A former first-round pick of the Wizards, JaVale McGee has found a home in his second year with the Warriors.

assists per game all while shooting 51.4 percent from the field and 46.3 percent from three-point range.

LATE-SEASON UPS AND DOWNS

The Warriors did scuffle a bit heading into the All-Star break in mid-February, clearly looking ahead to the time off even when there were still games to play, but they came out of the break reinvigorated, winning seven games in a row. This winning streak included a 32-point destruction of the Thunder at Oracle with Durant scoring 28 points while attacking Carmelo Anthony on defense, avenging the Warriors' two previous losses to the Thunder.

Durant also played a key role in the Warriors' March 8 win against the San Antonio Spurs, dominating the fourth quarter to give the Warriors the win. Unfortunately, that game was the start of a rather rough end of season for the Warriors. In that game Curry sprained his ankle again in the opening minutes. When Curry was finally healthy enough to return to the lineup on March 23 against the Atlanta Hawks, he suffered a Grade 2 MCL sprain that kept him out for the rest of the regular season.

With one of their core players sidelined for the rest of the regular season and nothing really to play for—as the Rockets had locked up the No. 1 seed while the Warriors were firmly entrenched in the No. 2 seed—the Warriors took their foot off the gas and seemingly coasted into the playoffs. There were some highs (an April 3 win in Oklahoma City with Durant scoring 34 points) and some scary moments (including Patrick McCaw's fall in the March 31 game against the Sacramento Kings), but by and large, what filled the rest of the Warriors' season was lackluster basketball. They lost by 20 points on the road to the Indiana Pacers.

"I'm embarrassed," Kerr said. "I know this game doesn't mean anything in the seeding, but the playoffs start next week. It was an embarrassing effort, pathetic effort."

The Warriors capped the regular season with an awful (yet meaningless) 40-point road loss to the Utah

Assistant coach Jarron Collins provides tutelage to rookie Jordan Bell, who already has become a valuable rotational player.

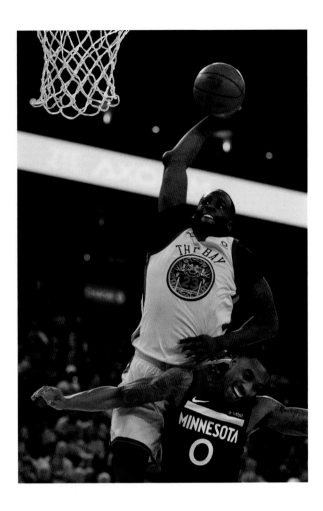

Jazz, bringing the 2017–18 regular season to an end—not with a bang, but a whimpering 7–10 stretch to close things out.

"There should always be a question in your mind if that switch is going to flip," Green said. "If anyone's capable of it, we are."

It was the rockiest, most uncomfortable and uncertain regular season that the Warriors have experienced in these past four seasons. And yet, after retaining possession of the Larry O'Brien Trophy and earning another championship banner to hang in Oracle Area, they proved that they were truly a team that could flip the switch when it mattered most. ■

Above: Draymond Green dunks over Timberwolves guard Jeff Teague during a 126–113 victory in January of 2018. Opposite: The Warriors' four All-Stars—Klay Thompson, Green, Kevin Durant, and Stephen Curry—show off their jerseys for the All-Star Game.

35

Small Forward

KEVIN DURANT

Prolific Shooter Adds Passing and Playmaking to His Game

Kevin Durant's second season with the Warriors was one of both highs and lows, setbacks and accomplishments.

Durant scored his 20,000th point in a 40-point performance against the Los Angeles Clippers, a game that the Warriors would ultimately lose. Durant's most prolific scoring exhibitions, including a 50-point performance against the Portland Trail Blazers, came in defeats.

Also, like most of the Warriors' roster, Durant dealt with his share of injury issues this season, missing 14 games due to a variety of ailments

When Durant played at his best in the 2017–18 season, it was when he displayed his talent in the other areas of basketball outside of scoring, and those abilities have really been allowed to shine in the Warriors' system.

In a win over the Minnesota Timberwolves on January 25, Durant finished the game with 11 assists after having 14 assists in his previous game against the New York Knicks. It was the first time in his career that Durant had back-to-back games with 10 or more assists. In that Timberwolves game, Durant had 10 rebounds to go with those 11 assists and 28 points to earn the 10th triple-double of his illustrious career.

One of Durant's opponents that night, the

Timberwolves' Jamal Crawford, had high words of praise for Durant.

"He's even more dangerous," Crawford said. "He's already the best scorer in the world. If he has the assists, that just makes it tough to deal with."

The nuances, particularly as a distributor and playmaker, the things in Durant's game that couldn't be seen when he was forced to shoulder so much of the load in Oklahoma City, continue to stand out for the All-Star forward.

Although these things are not totally new, Durant has been able to cultivate them and put them on fuller display since coming to the Warriors. Durant might have been the league's best scorer while playing for the Thunder, but coming to the Warriors has allowed him to be perhaps the league's best player.

Particularly during a stretch of games in December when Stephen Curry was out with a sprained ankle, Durant stepped up not only as a scorer, but also as a distributor and ball handler. Durant averaged nearly six assists per game in the month of December, a month in which Curry missed a significant amount of time. In 2017–18 Durant averaged 5.4 assists per game, basically mirroring the 5.5 assists he averaged during his 2013–14 MVP season.

Kevin Durant lays in two of his 25 points during the blowout victory in Game 3 of Western Conference Finals.

During that same stretch in December, Durant played some of the best defense of his career, averaging 2.5 blocks in the month. While this led to some ill-advised Defensive Player of the Year talk from many, including his teammate Draymond Green, Durant's defensive abilities have grown in his time with the Warriors, and he has been asked and been able to show more of what he can do on that side of the ball since coming to Golden State.

That said, Durant still turned in dominant scoring performances, showing why he is regarded as one of (if not the) best offensive weapons in the NBA right now.

"You think about a couple of years ago in the Finals we couldn't quite get over the hump," Warriors head coach Steve Kerr said about the 2017 Finals MVP. "Kevin is a guy that puts you over the hump. I don't know what you do to guard him. He can get any shot he wants."

One of those games in which Durant's ability to swing the outcome of a game through his scoring came against the San Antonio Spurs on March 8, a game in which Curry exited early with an ankle sprain. It was a back-and-forth game. The Spurs held an eight-point lead with 4:44 left in the game, which was punctuated by a Dejounte Murray dunk. At that point, it looked like the game might have finally slipped away from the Warriors. But the Warriors were not finished, thanks primarily to Durant.

Durant scored 12 consecutive Warriors' points after Murray's dunk. Durant tied the game at 105 with two minutes left to go, capping an amazing stretch for him. Durant was able to get whatever he wanted and completely exerted his will over the game. Durant finished that game against the Spurs with a game-high 37 points, including 15 in that remarkable fourth quarter.

"I felt good shooting the midrange as always," Durant said after the 110–107 win. "I tried to press, go, and shoot every time."

The up-and-down nature of Durant's season continued into the playoffs, as he would alternate between games in which he played well and then those where he struggled and became mired in isolation-heavy offense. But even with the struggles and difficulties of Durant's season, the way it ended for him and his team made up for it. And he continued to hone his impressive playmaking and defensive skills to go along with his otherworldly scoring. ∎

In a matchup of two of the best players in the NBA, Kevin Durant drives on LeBron James during the Warriors' win in Game 2 of the NBA Finals.

30

Point Guard

STEPHEN CURRY

Beautiful Moments Overcome an Injury-Plagued Regular Season

Stephen Curry's 2017–18 season was different than his past few namely because for the first time in many years he suffered through numerous injuries in the regular season that caused him to miss games. Curry played in just 51 games in the 2017–18 season, his lowest total since the 2011–2012 season. Though he dealt with recurring injuries throughout the season, Curry still averaged 26.4 points per game, shooting 49.5 percent from the field and 42.3 percent from three-point range. But even though Curry had yet another great year and was one of the two captains of the All-Star Game (along with LeBron James), what dominated his regular season were the injury concerns.

Curry suffered multiple sprains of his right ankle throughout the season, ranging from the mild to ones that kept him off the court for long stretches of the 2017–18 season.

The most painful one came on March 23 at home against the Atlanta Hawks, when he suffered a Grade 2 MCL sprain that kept him out of action for the rest of the regular season and the first round of the playoffs. This one was particularly painful, not only because of how long it kept Curry from playing, but also because he had worked so hard to come back from those previous injuries.

Warriors head coach Steve Kerr called it "a strange, cruel twist of fate. He rehabs his ankle for the last couple weeks, he gets that strong, and then the knee goes."

Without Curry in the lineup, the Warriors struggled offensively as the beautiful brand of basketball they normally play seemed to disappear. Though they still possessed a roster of remarkably talented players, the thing that made the Warriors special and unique wasn't there. The chemical reaction couldn't occur without Curry; he was the one that made that alchemy possible.

To see the magic that Curry brings to this team when he plays, one need not look further than the December 30 game against the Memphis Grizzlies, in which Curry returned from a right ankle sprain he suffered in a December 4 game against the New Orleans Pelicans that had kept him out of the previous 11 games.

Curry looked sharp from the opening tip of that game, which was amazing given how much time he had missed. Curry scored seven points. In the second quarter, the Warriors point guard really caught fire, scoring 14

Injuries sidelined Stephen Curry for some of the season, but he stepped up in in the Western Conference Finals.

points in the second to give him 21 points in the first half. Of those 14 points, nine came from long distance.

Curry scored a game-high 38 points, including a season-high 10 made three-pointers. (It was also Curry's ninth career game making more than 10 three-pointers, which is a NBA record.) That's particularly impressive, considering he missed more than three weeks of action while recovering from an injury.

"It felt like the first day of school again, for real," he said.

Just one night after playing stagnant offense against the Charlotte Hornets, the Warriors' offense looked turbo-charged against the Grizzlies, a team that ranked in the top 10 in opponent points per game at the time.

Kerr facetiously acknowledged the effect Curry had on the team.

"Everything just looks better," Kerr said. "The food in there is going to taste better tonight. My wife's going to be even better looking than she already is. My kids are going to be happy. Steph, he has that impact."

Curry's presence not only affects the team with the points he scores and the assists he makes, but also how he gives the team a special life and energy. The Warriors play faster, making more cuts, attacking the basket, and came onto the court with a greater focus and intensity. Curry not only puts in his own great performance, but he also elevates the games of his teammates as well.

"On offense it definitely picks the pace up," Kevin Durant said. "When he's out there, he's creating pace with his movement off the ball and in the pick-and-roll. Then you got two shooters in the corners with him and Draymond…and that just spreads the floor out for us even more."

The 2017-18 season was a trying one for Curry and the Warriors. While the Warriors' guard was not able to put up as many of the eye-popping numbers, there were moments like this late December game against Memphis when the two-time MVP's heroics and talent were on full display.

For Curry, the time when he truly shined was in the playoffs, and that magical play led the Warriors to their second consecutive NBA championship. ■

Stephen Curry exalts after outlasting the Cavaliers in overtime of Game 1 of the NBA Finals.

23

Power Forward

DRAYMOND GREEN

Once Again, Green Does All the Little Things

Draymond Green's 2017–18 season did not start out as he would have liked. Not only did his team drop their opening night game to the Houston Rockets, but Green was forced from the game with a strained left knee at the end of the third quarter. Without Green, the Warriors' defense fell apart, and the Rockets were able to get the win on the same night that the Warriors hung their 2016–17 championship banner.

After the MRI on his knee came back negative, Green (along with his Warriors teammates) could exhale.

"It was a big relief. I was concerned," Green said. "I honestly thought it was my meniscus."

It speaks to how particularly important Green is to this Warriors team that this felt like a major moment in the Warriors season, and it was only after one game.

The way we talk about Green and what he does for the Warriors has descended into cliché at this point, and yet that doesn't make those points any less true. Though his numbers don't dazzle and his play isn't as captivating, Green is an important piece of what makes the Warriors a great team.

Green led the Warriors in assists, rebounds, steals, and blocks, reflecting the different and diverse roles he plays for this team.

Green's coach (and occasional verbal sparring partner) Steve Kerr addressed Green's importance to this team and how great of a player he is.

"Obviously he's such a valuable player for us…a guy who fits the modern NBA so well," Kerr said. "You've got to be able to guard everybody on the floor and Draymond does that… The guy has huge energy, amazing defense, incredible basketball intellect. He's a future Hall of Famer. He's right in his prime right now, but this guy, he is the perfect modern-day NBA big. He can guard everybody. He can step out and make threes. He can handle the ball in transition…we're lucky to have him."

While Green did not win the Defensive Player of the Year award for the second straight season, it was still a good year for the forward as he continues to be one of the most unique players in the league today.

As has always been the case, Green plays some of his best games when the Warriors are going up against the best and toughest opponents. This is what happened on January 4 as the Warriors faced off against

Draymond Green, one of the best defenders in the NBA, tries to protect the rim while guarding LeBron James during Game 3 of the NBA Finals.

the Rockets, the team they would face in the Western Conference Finals.

With each team was missing players (the Rockets were without James Harden and the Warriors were without Stephen Curry), it was a challenging and hard-fought game that the Warriors won. Green was the spark and the driving force for the Warriors in that game.

Green finished the game with 10 assists, playing the role once again of Warriors chief facilitator. He also scored 17 points of his own in the matchup and contributed on the glass, pulling down 14 rebounds with 12 coming on the defensive end.

Green played good defense against the Rockets as well, picking up one of his two steals here early in the second quarter. Green was a game-high plus-16 against the Rockets, which reflects how the Warriors played at their best when he was on the court.

It was Green's 21st career triple-double and his second of three in the 2017–18 regular season. He is now the Warriors' franchise all-time leader in career triple-doubles.

But while Green had yet another solid regular season, he's played even better in the postseason. Green averaged close to a triple-double throughout the 2018 playoffs and did average one in the Western Conference Semifinals against the New Orleans Pelicans. It was the first time any Warriors player has averaged a triple-double in a playoff series.

While his teammates grab all the attention with their explosive offensive exploits, Green continues to do the smaller and less noticeable things to make this team a championship one. At this point in his career, Green has solidified himself as not only one of the best defenders in the NBA but also as one of the best all-around players. ■

He might not put up the glitzy numbers of his fellow All-Stars, but Draymond Green is one of the most integral players on the Warriors.

NEWCOMERS

JORDAN BELL, QUINN COOK, AND NICK YOUNG

New Roster Additions Play Role on Championship Squad

By and large, the Warriors brought back the same team that won the 2016–17 championship for the 2017–18 run. The core of the team remained fairly unchanged. However, around the margins, there were some new additions to this Warriors team, and they all came to the team through different means.

One of those new additions was rookie Jordan Bell from the University of Oregon. The Warriors did not have a pick in the 2017 NBA Draft but acquired the Chicago Bulls' pick in the second round (No. 38 overall) for cash considerations.

Bell showed a great deal of promise before the season even began, but many rookies have looked good in Summer League and the preseason. However, Bell's good play translated to the regular season, and it became clear that the Warriors had acquired a future rotation piece with that pick.

In a December 14 game against the Dallas Mavericks, Bell was inserted into the starting lineup due to injuries to Draymond Green and Zaza Pachulia. Given this surge in playing time, Bell took advantage and turned in a performance worthy of Green, the player whose game Bell's play most resembles and the player who has taken Bell under his wing.

The most eye-catching thing about Bell's performance in this early-season game were his eight assists, which was double his career high. Although Bell has shown his proficiency and potential as a passer occasionally this season, the rookie took it to another level in this game. Five of his assists came in the game's first half, meaning that Bell already reached his career high in assists after just one half of basketball.

Bell displayed a patience and feel of the game that one doesn't often see in a rookie. Rather than forcing up a shot with Dirk Nowitzki right in his face, Bell found Klay Thompson, who was able to take a better shot. It speaks to Bell being wise beyond his years, not making mistakes by forcing things, and looking for the higher percentage attempt.

Perhaps the least surprising thing about Bell's night was that his defense was strong yet again. Getting switched onto a guard like Wesley Matthews, Bell stayed down and didn't fall for any of his up fakes. Bell finished the game with six rebounds, including five on the defensive glass, and two steals, making contributions that allowed the Warriors to extend their early-season winning streak to eight games.

Unfortunately, Bell suffered multiple ankle injuries against the Bulls and Brooklyn Nets that limited how much of an impact he could have toward the end of the regular season.

"It's very frustrating, especially for me. I've never really had serious injuries," Bell said. "I've broken my

Jordan Bell, a second-round draft pick in the 2017 NBA Draft, receives instruction from head coach Steve Kerr during the Warriors' 127–108 victory against the Nuggets.

foot one time, but that was the only thing. I've never missed a basketball game since high school and college other than my foot being broken."

While Bell played well to start the Warriors' 2017–18 season, Quinn Cook was a new member of the Warriors roster who made an important contribution in the last month of the regular season. A starter on Duke's 2015 national championship team, Cook was initially signed to a two-way contract, meaning that he split time between the Warriors and their Santa Cruz G League affiliate.

But with Stephen Curry suffering an MCL injury that would sideline him for the rest of the regular season and Cook only able to play a limited amount of games with the club on that two-way contract, the Warriors ended up releasing free-agent signing Omri Casspi and signed Cook to a two-year contract.

Throughout the last month of the regular season, Cook took the injured Curry's place in the starting lineup, scoring more than 20 points in three straight games and even contributing 30 points in a loss to the Milwaukee Bucks.

One of those performances came in a March 19 game in San Antonio against the Spurs. Playing without Curry, Klay Thompson, and Kevin Durant and losing Draymond Green early in the game to injury, Cook kept things close for the Warriors and prevented the Spurs from running away with the win.

Cook finished that game with 20 points, five rebounds, and five assists while also providing the Warriors with offensive energy, as he pushed the ball up court and led the fast break. Though the Warriors lost the ugly 89–75 game, Cook kept things closer than they would have been otherwise and showed himself to be someone who could be a part of the Warriors' future plans.

Another player who helped out and contributed offense in that stretch of the season when the Warriors

Because of all of their injuries, the Warriors had to rely on players like (from left to right) Patrick McCaw, Nick Young, Jordan Bell, Shaun Livingston, and Kevon Looney.

were dealing with multiple injuries was Nick Young. Signed in the offseason, Young left the Los Angeles Lakers to come and play for a title with the Warriors.

Though he struggled to find consistent playing time in the Warriors' rotations, Young still managed to have an impact. Young scored 23 points in his first game with the Warriors during their opening night loss to the Houston Rockets. Young also scored 16 points in a February 24 matchup against the rival Oklahoma City Thunder and a season-high 24 points in the team's March 23 win against the Atlanta Hawks.

He even started Game 1 of the Western Conference Semifinals.

Though Young didn't always see extensive playing time, his presence was welcome with in the locker room. Reunited with JaVale McGee, his friend from his days with the Washington Wizards, the sometimes-inscrutable Swaggy P ingratiated himself with the championship core of this team.

Thus, after the Warriors won in Game 7 of the Western Conference Finals to advance to the NBA Finals, everyone on the team was happy for Young getting his chance to play in the NBA Finals. In fact the TNT broadcast crew wanted to interview him because it was his first time reaching that stage, but Young didn't have much use for the camera and microphone

"It means the world to me," he said. "I don't want to be interviewed right now. I want to go turn up. I really want to go have some fun, but you are interrupting my moment." ∎

While earning the start during an April victory, Quinn Cook, who scored 14 points, drives on Suns guard Tyler Ulis.

11

Shooting Guard

KLAY THOMPSON

Whether in the States or China, Thompson Thrives

The most important thing Klay Thompson did in the 2017–18 season might have occurred before the first game was played.

While traveling to China to promote his Anta brand basketball shoes, Thompson gave birth to one of the great basketball stories of recent memory.

Videos and pictures of Thompson appeared on Twitter under the #ChinaKlay hashtag showing the Warriors All-Star shooting guard dancing, drinking champagne, smoking cigars, playing basketball, and generally having the time of his life in the midst of a promotional tour of China.

Before the regular season began, his coach had some words of high praise for Thompson's life and his approach to things.

"If I could do it all over again, I would be Klay," Warriors head coach Steve Kerr said. "I mean that. I want to be Klay. He's got it figured out, just wants to play hoops and have fun and play with his dog. The most low maintenance guy on Earth."

Thompson was asked about #ChinaKlay after he returned to the United States.

"I didn't know it [would] go so viral when I was over there," he said. "I was just having a great time, but I forgot the Internet existed, so now I know."

While Thompson became a star on the Internet and captivated many a Twitter user, his on-the-court play was just as entertaining as his exploits in China.

Thompson averaged 20 points per game in the 2017–18 season, shooting 48.8 percent from the field and 42.2 percent from three-point range. Throughout the season Thompson showed that he was developing as a player and adding new things to his repertoire.

In addition to his abilities as a three-point shooter and a tenacious defender, Thompson showed strides as a passer as well as a ball handler. Thompson also did a better job driving to the basket in the 2017–18 season and not just settling for shots that he would have taken in seasons past.

One of Thompson's best games and where these newly developed traits were on full display came at the beginning of the season as the Warriors hosted the Toronto Raptors, a team that would go on to claim the best record in the Eastern Conference.

The Warriors shooting guard started the game with a first quarter three-pointer (not all that surprising) but coupled that with three assists (which was a bit more surprising). The Warriors roster is filled with

Klay Thompson makes a nifty no-look pass during the Warriors' 114–109 victory against the Hawks.

outstanding passers—Stephen Curry, Kevin Durant, Draymond Green, David West—but it was Thompson leading the team in assists at the end of the first.

The second quarter was when Thompson made his mark on the game, particularly through his scoring. He sank his second three-pointer of the night early in the quarter while also tallying his fourth assist.

A big night shooting the basketball is not that much of a surprise for Thompson, but seeing him set up teammates for a clear and easy dunk opportunity is a new wrinkle in his game.

While Thompson did not score as much in the third quarter as he did in the second, he continued to affect the game through his passing as well as his rebounding (grabbing two more in the quarter), making those watching wonder whether we'd see a triple-double, which has not happened yet in his seven-year career.

Thompson, like the rest of the Warriors, struggled down the stretch, allowing the Raptors to not only get back into the game but hold a five-point lead with a little over two minutes left to go in the game. But the shooting guard came up with big contributions to give the Warriors the win.

Thompson grabbed a key defensive rebound off of a Jakob Poeltl miss that led to a Curry layup to cut the Raptors' lead to three. Then, with the Warriors up by three and just seconds remaining, Thompson came up with another defensive play to seal the win. Thompson blocked Kyle Lowry's shot, getting the ball back to seal the game for the Warriors, who finished on a 10–0 run to claim the victory.

Thompson finished that Warriors win with 22 points (going an efficient 4-of-6 from three-point range) along with eight rebounds, five assists, one steal, and one block. Thompson's scoring was valuable not just to his team but to those throughout the Bay Area. During that homestand he promised to donate $1,000 for each point to the relief effort for the horrific fires in the North Bay Area.

Between his Internet fame from his trip to China and his continuing development as a player in this league, the 2017–18 season was an important one for Thompson, who has developed into, arguably, the best shooting guard in the NBA. ■

Klay Thompson drives on Pascal Siakam in a January victory when the Golden State shooting guard scored a team-high 26 points.

APRIL 14, 2018 | OAKLAND, CALIFORNIA
WARRIORS 113, SPURS 92

FLIPPING THE SWITCH
Warriors Turn Up Defensive Intensity, Klay Provides Offensive Fireworks

The Warriors started out their title defense in impressive fashion, blowing out the San Antonio Spurs 113–92 in the first game of the Western Conference Quarterfinals.

All season long, the Warriors played like a team that knew they were good, knew that the regular season would not be all that important, and knew that they should save their energy for the postseason. After a lackluster end of the regular season, questions arose if they could actually flip that proverbial switch and play like a championship team.

In their first game of the 2018 playoffs, the Warriors showed that they still had that extra gear and that they had been waiting for this moment to remind everyone just how good they could be.

Klay Thompson was the leading scorer for the Warriors, scoring 27 points and going 5-for-6 from three-point range. It was an efficient performance from Thompson, who took advantage of the open looks given to him by a scrambling Spurs defense. Although other players would see this kind of performance as remarkable, it was business as usual for Thompson. "I just try to play the same way at all times," the Warriors guard said. "It doesn't matter if I'm 11-for-13 or 2-for-13. I have the same mind-set."

Kevin Durant made his presence felt as well, scoring 24 points on an efficient 9-of-17 shooting. Shaun Livingston, picking up minutes with Stephen Curry sidelined with a sprained MCL, scored 11 points coming off of the bench.

With Curry still out of the lineup, the Warriors went with a bigger lineup to begin the game. Head coach Steve Kerr inserted JaVale McGee and Andre Iguodala into the starting lineup, playing McGee as the center while Iguodala served as the de facto point guard. Kerr's trust in McGee paid off as he scored 16 points and blocked two shots in 16 minutes of action.

But the benefits of this lineup extended well beyond their offensive play. Kerr described how this starting lineup choice was about "put[ting] our best defensive lineup on the floor from the beginning. I think the whole point of these games here early in this series is to re-establish our defense. Over the last month or so, our defense has been sub-par."

That lineup change had the intended effect as the Warriors played much better on the defensive side of the ball in Game 1.

The Warriors held Spurs All-Star LaMarcus Aldridge to just 14 points on 5-of-12 shooting. McGee's defending of Aldridge was particularly good, as he forced the Spurs forward into numerous contested or ill-advised shot attempts. Outside of Aldridge, only Rudy Gay and Bryn Forbes scored in double-digits. The Warriors also held the Spurs to 40 percent from the field—well below the 45.7 percent that they shot from the field in the regular season.

The Warriors also kept the Spurs off of the defensive glass, holding them to 27 defensive rebounds while grabbing 10 offensive rebounds of their own.

After a listless and unfocused end of the regular season, seeing the Warriors play with this kind of intensity—especially on defense—was a welcome sight and seemed to bode well for the rest of their postseason. ■

Klay Thompson points the way to victory in Game 1, in which he connected on 5-of-6 three-pointers.

WESTERN CONFERENCE QUARTERFINALS, GAME 2

APRIL 16, 2018 | OAKLAND, CALIFORNIA
WARRIORS 116, SPURS 101

SECOND-HALF SURGE

Warriors Storm Back Behind Klay's 24 Second-Half Points

In Game 2 of the Western Conference Quarterfinals, the Spurs put forth a much better effort than they did in Game 1, but a dominant second half performance by the Warriors gave them 116–101 victory.

Given how thoroughly the Warriors dominated in Game 1, many wondered whether the Spurs had any fight in them to make this a competitive series. In Game 2 the Spurs responded to those who doubted and underestimated them by giving the Warriors much more trouble in Game 1.

After his sub-par performance in Game 1, LaMarcus Aldridge became the target for much of that criticism from fans and media alike. The Spurs' All-Star forward played much better in Game 2, scoring 34 points and pulling down 12 rebounds. While JaVale McGee was able to consistently slow down Aldridge in Game 1, that was not the case for much of Game 2.

In addition to the Spurs playing better, the Warriors did not get off to a good start in Game 2. In the first half, they turned the ball over 11 times while also struggling from beyond the arc, shooting 30.8 percent as Kevin Durant missed all five of his three-point attempts. In Game 2 the Spurs presented a much more intense defensive effort, and that showed in the first half as they contained the Warriors' impressive offense and forced them into mistakes, which resulted in a six-point halftime lead for the visiting Spurs.

"It's hard to have a smooth game every game," Klay Thompson said, addressing the Warriors' ragged first half. "They were physical. Some of it was on us. But giving them credit, they came out and responded very well after the last game."

The second half of Game 2 was a much better one for the Warriors as they outscored the Spurs by 21 points on their way to another blowout victory.

At the heart of the Warriors' second half surge in Game 2 was Thompson, who scored 24 of his points in the second half, getting hot and going 4-of-6 from three-point range. Thompson's three-point shooting fueled the Warriors' second-half run along with Kevin Durant and his 15 second-half points (11 of which came in the third quarter).

"[Thompson] hit some tough shots off one leg, and you know had some opportunity bounces," Aldridge said after the game. "That's why they are who they are. They made tough shots. KD made tough shots."

Although the Warriors' offense was a bit stagnant in the first half, their second-half fluidity and ball movement was on display, showing up in the Warriors' 19 second-half assists (including five from Durant).

After winning the first two games of this series by a combine 36 points, the Warriors looked to be in full and complete control of this opening-round matchup. ■

Klay Thompson drives the ball against Spurs guard Patty Mills, but it was from the perimeter where he really did his damage.

APRIL 19, 2018 | SAN ANTONIO, TEXAS
WARRIORS 110, SPURS 97

DRAYMOND DOMINATES ON D

Green's All-Around Effort Stymies Grieving Spurs

After the series' first two games in Oakland, things shifted to San Antonio where the Warriors defeated the Spurs 110–97.

It was a game whose energy was tempered by the news that the wife of Spurs coach Gregg Popovich had passed away. Given the close relationship between Popovich and Warriors head coach Steve Kerr, both locker rooms were thinking of the longtime Spurs coach, who did not coach in Game 3.

Once again, the Warriors' defensive effort was the biggest factor in their victory. Though facing a team limited offensively with the absence of Kawhi Leonard, the Warriors' defense played exceedingly well in their Game 3 victory. They prevented any Spurs player from scoring more than 20 points and held them to 21.2 percent from three-point range. Draymond Green led the defensive charge for the Warriors, blocking four Spurs shots and getting two steals to go with his 10 points, seven assists, and six rebounds.

"He's been fantastic defensively, all over the place," head coach Steve Kerr said after the game. "This is a team that you have to disrupt. They're excellent with their execution until you have to try to take them out of things, and Draymond is as good as anybody I've ever seen in terms of recognizing a play and blowing it up."

Kevin Durant stepped up once again to power the Stephen Curry-less Warriors' offense, scoring 26 points, six assists, and nine rebounds. After his stellar performance in the first two games of this series, Klay Thompson struggled in Game 3, scoring just 19 points. Shaun Livingston and Quinn Cook, both seeing more playing time due to Stephen Curry's absence, scored 16 and 12 points, respectively, off the bench.

That said, the Warriors offense did have its fair share of struggles in this game, particularly in the first half. After shooting 48.4 percent from three-point range in Game 2, the Warriors struggled from distance to start Game 3. In the first half, they shot 9.1 percent from three-point range, which is remarkably abysmal for a great shooting team like the Warriors.

The Warriors didn't make their first three-pointer of the game until there was just a little over two minutes left in the first half, when Klay Thompson finally knocked one down.

Though they still led at halftime and were making their shots from two-point range at a pretty consistent rate (51.2 percent in the first half), their lack of success from long distance allowed the Spurs to stay in this game. The Warriors' offense picked up in the second half, allowing them to put some distance between them and the Spurs.

Part of an impressive defensive effort in Game 3, (from left to right) Draymond Green, Klay Thompson, and Kevin Durant surround Spurs big man LaMarcus Aldridge.

The game was also punctuated by a couple of close calls that had Warriors fans holding their breath. Both Durant and Livingston twisted their left ankles in the fourth quarter, causing them to exit the game and go back to the AT&T Center locker room. Neither resulted in a serious injury, but for a fanbase that had witnessed far too many injuries over the past season, it elicited a moment of anxiety.

Even though they'd struggled at times, both in this game and series, the Warriors now had a commanding advantage in the Western Conference Quarterfinals and looked to potentially sweep their opening-round opponents. ∎

WESTERN CONFERENCE QUARTERFINALS, GAME 4
APRIL 22, 2018 | SAN ANTONIO, TEXAS
SPURS 103, WARRIORS 90

THROWING ONE AWAY

Early Turnovers Sink Warriors' Quest for a Sweep

In their quest to sweep their opening-round series, the Warriors came up short as they dropped Game 4 to the San Antonio Spurs 103–90.

From the very beginning of Game 4, it was clear that the Warriors focus had wandered since they had so clearly asserted that they were the better team in the previous three games. Turnovers, the Warriors' biggest issue throughout the regular season, returned in a big way during Game 4. They committed seven turnovers in the first five minutes of Game 4, which set the tone for how this game was going to go for the Warriors.

"The ballgame was the first quarter," said Shaun Livingston after the game, "the first five minutes."

For the first few games of this opening-round series, the Warriors had been careful with the ball and didn't make the same sloppy turnovers that were omnipresent in the regular season. But in Game 4, they turned the ball over 16 times, something that one can't do against a team like the Spurs.

The Warriors' turnovers were particularly costly because the Spurs' offense played well for the first time in the series. One of the worst three-point shooting teams in the regular season, the Spurs shot 53.6 percent from beyond the arc in Game 4. LaMarcus Aldridge went 3-of-3 from long distance on his way to 22 points, which included a couple desperation three-point shots with the shot clock winding down that miraculously went in.

Much like Livingston, Draymond Green pointed to the Warriors' bad start as to why those Spurs shots were so costly.

"You get in such a hole and then you're playing the right way, you're doing all the right things, you're doing everything you need to get over the hump," he said. "But one call doesn't go your way, one bounce doesn't go your way, one shot like that doesn't go your way, and that's where everything catches up to you."

In addition to Aldridge, the Warriors had to contend with Manu Ginobili, who turned back the clock with a vintage performance. Coming off of the bench, the veteran scored 16 points in 25 minutes of action.

While the Spurs' offense played its best game, the Warriors' offense slowed to a crawl in Game 4. Kevin Durant scored 34 points, but it took him 28 shots to get there. Klay Thompson scored just 12 points, and the only other Warriors player in double-digits scoring was Livingston. Above all, the Warriors weren't moving the ball, managing only 19 assists as a team, forcing them into an isolated-based offense and bad shots. ∎

Like the rest of his teammates, Klay Thompson has trouble holding onto the ball during Game 4. The Warriors committed 18 turnovers in the loss.

APRIL 24, 2018 | OAKLAND, CALIFORNIA
WARRIORS 99, SPURS 91

TO THE SEMIFINALS

Draymond Hauls in 19 Boards to Close Out Spurs

The Warriors closed out their first-round series against the San Antonio Spurs with a workmanlike 99–91 victory at Oracle Arena. While Klay Thompson contributed 24 points and Kevin Durant scored 25, including the basket that sealed the win, the Golden State Warriors won Game 5 because of everything that Draymond Green did.

Green scored 17 points in Game 5, his best scoring effort since a game in mid-March game against the Phoenix Suns. As one would have expected, the All-Star forward has become much more aggressive on offense in the playoffs, particularly because teams are giving Green open looks at three-pointers, choosing to funnel their defenses toward Thompson and Durant instead.

Though he didn't shoot for a great percentage in Game 5, Green is still taking shots that he might have passed up in the regular season. The important thing is for Green to take those open shots because, eventually, they start to fall and they maintain the team's offensive rhythm.

Green picked up where he left off in Game 4 with his rebounding. After grabbing 18 rebounds in Game 4, Green was one better and had 19 rebounds in Game 5. Most notably, five of Green's rebounds were on the offensive glass, which gave the Warriors multiple opportunities to score. Green also had 14 defensive rebounds against the Spurs, pulling down more rebounds on defense than LaMarcus Aldridge did in total.

"One thing we spoke about coming into this series was trying to control the glass," Green said after the game, "Crash the offensive boards, then made sure we finished our possessions on the defensive end."

Green played like the reigning NBA Defensive Player of the Year in Game 5 and provided the spark on that side of the ball to get the series-clinching victory.

Green contested on numerous Spurs shots and defended players, ranging from bigs like Aldridge to wings like Rudy Gay to small guards like Patty Mills, displaying that defensive versatility that makes him such a unique player and a difficult one to play against.

As a team, the Spurs shot 37.2 percent from the field largely because of the defensive pressure Green put on them. Not surprisingly, the Spurs' three-point shooting came back to Earth, as they shot 23.3 percent one game after their jaw-dropping 53.6 percent rate from long distance in Game 4.

"Draymond can literally do everything," Thompson said, "So these last two games, he's been rebounding like a beast. And his ability to take the ball from the rim and push the break is what sparks the offense so much."

While Durant and Thompson were important contributors, Green displayed his all-around game in Game 5 as well as the intensity he brings when there's a chance to close out an opponent. Because of Green, the Warriors were able to dispatch the Spurs and move on to the next round of the playoffs. ∎

Tony Parker and the Spurs couldn't contain Draymond Green, who had 19 rebounds in the Game 5 victory.

APRIL 28, 2017 | OAKLAND, CALIFORNIA
WARRIORS 123, PELICANS 101

OFFENSIVE EXPLOSION

41-Point Second Quarter Leads to Blowout, Draymond Records Triple-Double

After playing against San Antonio Spurs, a team that looked to slow down the pace, in the first round of the Western Conference playoffs, the Warriors faced a team—the New Orleans Pelicans—in the semifinals that wanted to play at a much faster clip.

In their 123–101 Game 1 win against the Pelicans at Oracle Arena, the Warriors showed that they could still win in a shootout and boasted an equally impressive offense to go with their stifling defense.

"Our guys love playing this style," head coach Steve Kerr said after the game. "[O]nce we settled in and we established our defense, I think our guys were excited. They like this pace."

It came as a bit of a shock after that first-round matchup with the Spurs. Draymond Green attested to this, describing how "Klay [Thompson] looked at me at one point on the bench and said, 'Man, Draymond, I got more tired tonight than I did in any game against the Spurs.' That kind of sums it up; it's a completely different tempo. They are really pushing the ball, like he said, and nonetheless, as long as we are getting back into transition and not giving up easy stuff, I think that plays into our hands."

Exhaustion aside, the Warriors looked very comfortable playing at this fast tempo, scoring a 2018 postseason high (to that point) of 123 points while also recording 33 assists in the Game 1 win. Thompson led the way for the Warriors with 27 points, while Kevin Durant added 26 points of his own. Green, meanwhile, scored 16 points while handing out 11 assists and grabbing 15 rebounds for the 26th triple-double of his NBA career. Twelve of Green's points and 10 of his rebounds came in the first half alone.

It was an impressive offensive first half for the Warriors, as they scored 35 points in the first quarter and 41 in the second (while holding the Pelicans to just 21 points in that second quarter). The offensive exploits of the Warriors electrified the crowd at Oracle Arena, as Kerr noted "it was probably the loudest I've heard Oracle all year." The Warriors' ability to hit the ground running also allowed them to bury the Pelicans early and win this game going away.

Fresh off of their first-round domination of the Portland Trail Blazers, the Pelicans could not keep things going. A large part of that was the Warriors' defense on Anthony Davis, specifically the play of Kevon Looney. Davis scored 21 points on 9-of-20 shooting—not enough for the Pelicans to keep up with a championship team like the Warriors. After being such a dominant force in the first round, Davis was contained in the first game of this second-round matchup, and thus the Pelicans struggled.

With Stephen Curry still sidelined, Kerr again

Draymond Green, who helped limit Anthony Davis to 9-of-20 shooting, blocks a pass intended for the Pelicans star.

made another starting lineup change as Nick Young was inserted into the starting lineup alongside Durant, Thompson, Green, and Andre Iguodala. Young went 2-of-4 from the field, all from three-point range, and ended the game with six points. Against the Spurs it made sense to go with a bigger, longer, and more defensively-oriented lineup. Against the fast-paced Pelicans, Kerr elected to go with speed and shooting, and that paid off in the 22-point win.

The Warriors were able to get the 1–0 advantage in the series while also knowing that Curry's return to the lineup was just around the corner. But the Warriors had to feel good that they were able to get this kind of an offensive performance even without their two-time MVP on the court. ■

Opposite: Kevon Looney uses his long frame to help defend Anthony Davis. Above: Shaun Livingston, who scored 10 points off the bench, scoops the ball onto the glass past Davis.

WESTERN CONFERENCE SEMIFINALS, GAME 2

MAY 1, 2018 | OAKLAND, CALIFORNIA
WARRIORS 121, PELICANS 116

HE'S BACK

Curry Returns to Action, Scores 28 Points in 27 Minutes

The moment Warriors fans—and all those who enjoy magnificent basketball—had been waiting for had finally arrived. Stephen Curry returned from his sprained MCL to the Warriors lineup in Game 2 of the Western Conference Semifinals, playing an important role in the 121–116 victory that gave the Warriors a 2–0 series lead over the New Orleans Pelicans in this second-round series.

Though he came off of the bench in this first game back in action, Curry managed to have the same impact on the game that he would have if he was starting. Curry scored 28 points in 27 minutes, including going 5-of-10 from three-point range. Entering the game in the first quarter with the Warriors trailing 19–11, Curry hit a deep three-pointer after being on the court just 11 seconds.

"We call a play we like to run just to get some movement, just to get the ball moving, and the ball swung to him, and he just launched," head coach Steve Kerr said, "didn't surprise me. That's who he is. That was a fun moment."

The Warriors needed Curry and his offense because—unlike Game 1—the Pelicans kept up with them in the first half. The Warriors led by just three points at halftime before extending their lead to 13 points with less than two minutes left to go in the game. Through sloppy play and ill-advised shots, the Warriors allowed the Pelicans to cut into that lead before the final buzzer sounded to end the game.

The Warriors' other major offensive weapons, Klay Thompson and Kevin Durant, both struggled while Curry shined. Thompson has just 11 points on 4-of-20

shooting while Durant had 29 points but had issues for most of the game with his three-point shot, going 2-of-7 from long distance.

"I was rushing a little bit too much and then I missed a few trying to find it so quickly," Durant said. "But I just tried to slow down in the fourth, and my teammates did a good job of slowing the pace for me and finding me in the post and moving off the ball, as well, to give me some space to work, and I was able to knock some shots down."

In the fourth quarter, however, Durant started to play better as he scored 15 points and sealed the Warriors' victory while the Pelicans tried to mount one last run.

Draymond Green continued his excellent playoffs, scoring 20 points to go with his 12 assists and nine rebounds in Game 2. Once again, Green's defense was also outstanding as he, along with Kevon Looney, did their best against the formidable Pelicans frontcourt.

After his pedestrian performance in Game 1, Anthony Davis responded with an impressive 25-point, 15-rebound game. The Pelicans also got big games from Rajon Rondo (22 points, 12 assists) and Jrue Holiday (24 points, eight assists, eight rebounds). But that was not enough to overtake a surging Warriors with the help of the returning Curry.

Being up 2–0 in the series and with their two-time MVP back, the Warriors seemed poised to once again put an overmatched opponent into an insurmountable hole and swiftly move on to the next series in these 2018 playoffs. ∎

Stephen Curry's return from injury in Game 2 provided a huge lift for the Warriors.

The Warriors' faithful cheer on Stephen Curry as he scores the first of his 28 points.

MAY 4, 2018 | NEW ORLEANS, LOUISIANA
PELICANS 119, WARRIORS 100

BROW BEATEN

Dominant Davis Helps Limit Lackluster Dubs to 38 Percent Shooting

The Warriors did a pretty good job defending Anthony Davis in the first two games of the Western Conference Semifinals. In Game 3 at the Smoothie King Center in New Orleans, Davis showed why he is a MVP candidate with his performance during a dominant 119–100 Pelicans win that gave them their first win of the series.

Davis scored 33 points in the Pelicans' Game 3 win while also pulling in 18 rebounds and playing like he had in the Pelicans' opening-round matchup against the Trail Blazers.

Part of why Davis was able to have such a productive night was because of the Warriors' decision to start JaVale McGee at the center position. While Kevon Looney had been playing well against Davis, McGee was no match for Davis, and the Pelicans' big man took full advantage.

Davis also led a defensive effort that stifled a Warriors offense that had looked dominant in the first two games of the series, ending the night with four steals of his own. In Game 3 the Warriors shot 38 percent from the field and 29 percent from three-point range. Klay Thompson led the Warriors with 26 points but on 9-of-22 shooting, an inefficiency indicative of the rough night the Warriors had on offense.

The Warriors' defensive effort in Game 3 left much to be desired as well. The other, non-Davis Pelicans players were able to thrive because of that. Jrue Holiday put in another good performance in this series as he scored 21 points despite being guarded by Kevin Durant for much of the game. Former Warriors guard Ian Clark came off of the bench and contributed 18 points of his own while Rajon Rondo ended the game with 21 assists.

In his second game back from injury, Stephen Curry came back to Earth after his show-stopping display in Game 2. Curry scored 19 points on 6-of-19 shooting in Game 3 and showed some of the rust that emerged from missing so much time from injury.

"I was rushing a little bit and just missed shots," Curry said. "I'm not going to get in my head about it. You can't really dwell on anything."

While unlucky bounces and abnormally bad shooting were one reason for the Warriors' poor performance, head coach Steve Kerr was quick to point to another reason for his team's Game 3 loss.

"Most of it is attributed to the Pelicans. Their defense was great," the Warriors coach said after the game. "They were the aggressors. They brought the necessary force to the game on their home floor, and these are the ebbs and flows of the playoffs."

Whether because of bad luck, poor effort, or an inspired opponent, the Warriors lost Game 3 and gave the Pelicans some life in this series.

"They did whatever they wanted," Thompson said. "We have to come back on Sunday and make them more uncomfortable because they were way too comfortable." ∎

Pelicans guard Jrue Holiday fouls Stephen Curry, who came back to Earth a bit in Game 3, following his impressive performance in Game 2.

Anthony Davis protects the rim as part of his monster, 33-point, 18-rebound performance in Game 3.

WESTERN CONFERENCE SEMIFINALS, GAME 4

MAY 6, 2018 | NEW ORLEANS, LOUISIANA
WARRIORS 118, PELICANS 92

HAMPTONS 5 COMES ALIVE

Durant Scores 38, Warriors Go Up 3–1 on Pelicans

After dropping Game 3 to the New Orleans Pelicans, head coach Steve Kerr decided to put his best foot forward in Game 4. He started the Hamptons 5.

The result? A 118–92 blowout that put the Warriors just one win away from a fourth straight trip to the Western Conference Finals.

Coined by The Athletic's Tim Kawakami, the nickname refers to Kevin Durant and the four members of the Warriors roster (Stephen Curry, Klay Thompson, Draymond Green, and Andre Iguodala) who courted him in The Hamptons in the summer of 2016.

In the pre-Durant era with Harrison Barnes filling that role, this lineup was known as the Death Lineup, and Kerr's implementation of it was an enormous factor in the Warriors winning the 2015 championship and Iguodala winning Finals MVP.

The athleticism present in the lineup makes it a very difficult team to attack because of their ability to switch and make smart defensive plays. Meanwhile, the shot-making potential, the speed at which all five players can play, and the high basketball IQ present makes them an exceedingly difficult group to guard.

Starting this vaunted lineup had the intended effect as the Warriors were in control from the beginning of the game, busting out with a 17–4 run rather than falling behind and needing to catch up. Though the Pelicans would make runs throughout the game, they could not make any meaningful headway in cutting the deficit and suffered a 26-point loss.

Durant seemed to be enlivened by Kerr's choice to put out the best lineup out from the opening tip, as he scored 38 points while also having nine rebounds and five assists in Game 4.

"You could just tell that very first play, the way he came off that dribble handoff, where his mind-set was at," Green said about Durant's performance.

"I just try to tell myself that I'm at my best when I don't care what happens," Durant said. "That's when I'm free and having fun out there, and forceful. That was the thing—just try to play with force, no matter if I missed shots or not, just keep shooting, keep being aggressive."

While Durant and Curry (23 points) were dazzling, Iguodala did the little and oft-overlooked things to make sure the Warriors got the victory. Playing in the starting lineup alongside the Warriors' four All-Stars, Iguodala had six points, six assists, seven rebounds, three steals, one block, and no turnovers.

Andre Iguodala, who also had seven rebounds and six assists, throws down a dunk during the Game 4 win.

After the game, Kerr had words of high praise for Iguodala, comparing him to one of the head coach's former teammates.

"He reminds me a lot of Scottie Pippen," Kerr said, "in terms of defensive acumen and playing kind of a point forward role. Andre's amazing."

In addition to jump-starting the Warriors' offense, the lineup change also had a similar effect on their defensive effort. The Warriors held the Pelicans to 36.4 percent shooting from the field while limiting Anthony Davis to 26 points on 8-of-22 shooting. In Game 4 the Warriors forced 19 Pelicans turnovers, including six by Davis and four by Rajon Rondo.

Kerr's decision to lead with the Hamptons 5 paid off in a big way and has the Warriors on the precipice of moving onto the Western Conference Finals and, hopefully, another berth in the NBA Finals. ∎

As part of Draymond Green's excellent five-steal, two-block defensive performance, he pestered E'Twaun Moore around the rim all game long.

WESTERN CONFERENCE SEMIFINALS, GAME 5
MAY 8, 2018 | OAKLAND, CALIFORNIA
WARRIORS 113, PELICANS 104

GANG GREEN

Draymond, Steph, Klay, and KD Push Warriors on to the Conference Finals

The Warriors finished off the New Orleans Pelicans in Game 5 of the Western Conference Semifinals, winning Game 5 at Oracle Arena 113–104. The win came largely because of the performance of the Warriors' marquee players, but it was the occasionally overlooked one who played the biggest role in the Warriors' victory.

While the Golden State Warriors' other All-Stars—Stephen Curry (28 points and eight assists), Klay Thompson (23 points), and Kevin Durant (24 points)—all had excellent games, Draymond Green's performance in Game 5 propelled the Warriors to the series-clinching win and continued his outstanding 2018 postseason.

Green finished Tuesday night's game with 19 points, 14 rebounds, and nine assists, falling just short of another triple-double. But Green still averaged a triple-double in the Western Conference Semifinals, which is the first time a Warriors player has ever averaged a triple-double for a playoff series.

Green scored eight of his 19 points in the fourth quarter. As the Pelicans went on an extended run in the fourth to pull within seven points—after trailing by 26 points at one point—Green hit the important shot with just under two minutes left in the game to stop the Warriors' bleeding. As Curry, Thompson, and Durant all went cold from the field down the stretch, Green provided just enough of an offensive push to keep the Pelicans at bay and secure the Warriors' series-clinching victory.

The Warriors' ball movement in Game 5 was stellar as they tallied 36 assists, and Green's nine were the most of any Warriors player. In the Western Conference Semifinals, Green averaged 10 assists per game and did not have fewer than nine assists in any of the five games against the Pelicans. While the Warriors offense looked a big ragged at times in the opening round series against the Spurs, in the Western Conference Semifinals, they looked more like the Warriors we're used to watching as the ball moved around and found the open man.

Not surprisingly, Green was the focal point of the Warriors defense, particularly in dealing with Anthony Davis. It is no easy task, but Green handled it about as well as anyone could. Though Davis finished with 34 points, Green made sure he had to work for every one of those points.

"Our guys have brought it," head coach Steve Kerr said, regarding his team's defensive effort. "They have brought the energy, the juice, the awareness, and we have a team that can defend a lot of different styles, and that's important in the playoffs because you see a lot of different teams obviously."

That said, there are still issues that the Warriors must address. While Curry has looked better, he's still making his way not just into playing shape but playoffs shape.

"I feel confident with what I'm able to do out there," Curry said after the win. "After being out six weeks, I just appreciate being out there and playing."

It was another brilliant performance in a closeout game from Green and, along with the contributions of his fellow teammates, the Warriors finished off the Pelicans and made their way to the Western Conference Finals. ∎

Draymond Green boxes out Anthony Davis. That effort helped the Warriors outrebound the Pelicans 52–44.

Springy forward Andre Iguodala uses his athleticism to snare a first-half rebound during Golden State's Game 5 victory.

WESTERN CONFERENCE FINALS, GAME 1

MAY 14, 2018 | HOUSTON, TEXAS
WARRIORS 119, ROCKETS 106

FLIPPING HOMECOURT

Durant, Warriors Seize Control in Dominant Third Quarter

It was finally here—the matchup the entire regular season was building toward. The Golden State Warriors and Houston Rockets were playing in Western Conference Finals, starting with Game 1 at the Toyota Center in Houston.

The game went back and forth for much of the first half with both teams shooting well from the field, but the Warriors put together a dominant second half on their way to a 119–106 win.

In what has become a staple of these Warriors teams, it was another impressive third quarter that broke the halftime tie and allowed the visitors to seize control of the game. The Warriors outscored the Rockets 31–24 in the third quarter, leading by as many as 13 points. Leading the way for the Warriors was Kevin Durant, who scored 13 of his 37 points in the third.

What became clear in that third quarter is that the Rockets had no defensive answer for Durant, no way to slow him down. The Warriors knew that if they could get the ball to Durant, he could get a good look at a shot. Even with Durant rolling, Warriors head coach Steve Kerr elected to sit Durant down to get his All-Star forward some rest, to which Durant responded with an incredulous, "Why?" After the substitution the Rockets went on a quick run, and Kerr got Durant back in the game to steady things.

"Kevin's never happy when he comes out of the game, no matter when I take him out," Kerr said. "Even in the preseason, he's upset if I take him out."

The Warriors defense was also strong in that important third quarter, holding the high-powered Rockets to just 24 points. The Warriors withstood the Rockets' best punch as they jumped out to an early nine-point lead in the first quarter.

This is where the Warriors really demonstrated their playoff experience and championship poise. In Game 1 the Warriors again showed their ability to overcome fast starts by teams and gradually wrestle control of a game.

Monday night displayed both the good and the frustrating aspects of Draymond Green. The more vexing parts of Green's game came early on, specifically when he picked up an early technical foul for shoving James Harden.

From the opening tip, it was clear that Green was playing with a ton of energy. That excess energy came back to bite him as he picked up three fouls in the first half, sending him to the bench with four minutes left in the second quarter. After Green went to the bench, the Warriors defense struggled, and the Rockets were able to erase the Warriors' six-point advantage and get things tied up by halftime.

"I was a bit overzealous, a bit amped up," Green said after the game. "But I'd rather that any day than coming out flat."

As the game progressed, that initial burst of superfluous energy disappeared, and Green settled down

Part of a stout defensive performance, Klay Thompson and Draymond Green harass Rockets forward Trevor Ariza.

into playing his normal, fiery game and thus he began to have a positive impact on Monday night's game.

Green finished with five points, nine rebounds, nine assists, two steals, and two blocks. As is often the case with Green, the high caliber of his performance does not show up in the traditional statistical measures, particularly because so much of what he does is on defense and thus hard to quantify

Green did a great job contesting shots on the perimeter as well as in the paint. Whether it was blocking a P.J. Tucker three-point attempt or battling for rebounds with Clint Capela, Green did it all in Game 1.

Game 1 was an impressive top-to-bottom performance for the Warriors as they got contributions from several people on their roster. Klay Thompson was the other hot hand on offense, along with Durant, as he scored 28 points while going 6-of-15 from three-point range.

Three of Thompson's makes from beyond the arc came in the fourth quarter as the Rockets tried to mount one last run to make a game of it. But Thompson was able to get open and knocked down those open shots to put the proverbial nail in the coffin.

Asked if he remembered a game when he was able to get that open, Thompson responded: "In the playoffs? Not too many."

While Durant and Thompson provided the Warriors' offensive punch, Stephen Curry struggled in Game 1. The Warriors point guard was particularly off from long distance, going 1-of-5 from three-point range. Between coming back from the MCL sprain and having the Rockets direct most of their offensive attack at him, it's perhaps not surprising that Curry struggled to get into a groove.

However, Curry did finish with 18 points in large part because he made a point of attacking the basket. Curry also finished Monday night's game with eight assists and, most impressive of all, just one turnover.

Though he did not wow with the offensive exploits to which we've all become so accustomed, Curry picked his spots and played an important role in this Warriors' road win.

As Kerr had alluded to in the days leading up to this first game, Nick Young received minutes against the Rockets. The Warriors' reserve guard made the most of his time on the court, scoring nine points while shooting 3-of-5 from three-point range in 15 minutes of action.

Kevon Looney also ended up playing some major minutes in Monday night's game. Looney played 25 minutes in Game 1 and, though his stat line wasn't particularly impressive, he still did about as well as one could out there. He didn't stop Harden or Chris Paul every time he was switched on him, but he held his own. It was a solid performance by Looney, and the Warriors hope they'll continue to see that effort as the series moves forward.

On the whole, the Warriors did their best defending Harden. But given that he's such a great player, it's hard to truly limit Harden. That was definitely the case on Monday night as Harden finished the game with 41 points on 14-of-24 shooting. But those big numbers for Harden might have been, to some degree, by design for the Warriors.

Forcing Harden to be so ball dominant and dictate everything in these isolation-heavy situations clearly wore him out. Harden had all four of his turnovers in Game 1 in the second half as he'd had to expend so much energy, which led to him making careless or not-so-smart plays.

While Harden and, to a lesser degree, Paul were able to score, no other Rockets player could get anything consistently going offensively. After one game, the Warriors took homecourt advantage away from the Rockets and got the important first win in the Western Conference Finals. ∎

Andre Iguodala dunks the ball in the second half—the portion of Game 1 when the Warriors pulled away.

MAY 16, 2018 | HOUSTON, TEXAS
ROCKETS 127, WARRIORS 105

ROCKETS RESPOND

P.J. Tucker, Rockets Defeat Turnover-Prone Warriors

After their impressive Game 1 victory, the Warriors looked to take a commanding series lead in the Western Conference Finals on Wednesday night. For the Rockets Game 2 was a must-win game as they desperately needed to salvage a split in these initial home games.

Not surprisingly, the Rockets played with desperation and intensity while the Warriors, for long stretches at least, looked like a team content to head back home. That was evident in the game's final score as the Rockets blew out the Warriors, winning 127–105 to even up the Western Conference Finals at one game apiece.

Although the Warriors were poised and in control to begin this series, they did not start Game 2 in a similar fashion. Gone was the team that looked like it had flipped the switch and had a laser-like focus on the task at hand. In its place was the Warriors team we saw during stretches of the regular season, displaying a proclivity for turning the ball over and making careless plays.

In the first half, the Warriors had 11 turnovers while they had nine total turnovers in Game 1. The Rockets took advantage of those Warriors turnovers, converting them into the fast break points that they were unable to get in Game 1.

While the Warriors are well-equipped to overcome slow starts and take a team's best punch, the poor start to Game 2 was a particularly unfortunate one. The Warriors had the Rockets somewhat on the ropes after that impressive Game 1 victory. By turning the ball over and allowing the Rockets to get their offense up and running, the Warriors gave confidence to a team in desperate need of it.

Another issue for the Warriors was poor shooting, especially from three-point range. The Warriors shot an abysmal 30 percent from long distance in Game 2 and didn't make their first three-pointer until the second quarter.

Stephen Curry had a particularly rough night, shooting 1-of-8 from three-point range and not making that first three-pointer until late in the game. Curry scored just 16 points (though he also had seven assists) as he looked ever-so-slightly off for the second straight game.

"First game, I did a lot better," Curry said, reflecting on his two performances in the 2018 Western Conference Finals. "Stats-wise, it looked the same. But I played a lot more decisively, a lot more aggressively."

But it wasn't just Curry who struggled offensively. Klay Thompson scored just eight points, taking quite a few bad shots while not getting the same open looks he saw during Game 1. Draymond Green looked hesitant to shoot, which led to him overpassing and thus leading to more turnovers. David West missed quite a few baskets from point-blank range during his six minutes of playing time, as he continues to struggle against this Rockets team.

The only Warriors player who could get anything

Clint Capela, who had 10 rebounds in Game 2, shoots over Shaun Livingston as the Rockets even the Western Conference Finals at 1–1.

THE BRILLIANCE OF THE 2018 CHAMPION GOLDEN STATE WARRIORS

going offensively was Kevin Durant, who scored 38 points on Wednesday night, one more than his Game 1 output. Again, the Rockets didn't seem to have a defensive answer for Durant and appeared to be employing a similar strategy to what the Warriors did with James Harden in Game 1. The Rockets were comfortable with Durant getting whatever he wanted—as long as they shut down everyone else.

The Rockets deserve a great deal of credit for the Warriors' offensive woes. They looked better and more energized defensively on Wednesday night. But the Warriors missed a lot of shot they usually knock down.

"That's the beauty of the game, man," Durant said after the final whistle. "Some games, you're going to get knocked out. Some games, you're going to get punched in the face. How you respond? That's the beauty of it."

Although Harden had a strong game (27 points, 10 rebounds) and Chris Paul came up with some baskets in crucial moments, perhaps the biggest reason for the Rockets' Game 2 win was the performance of their supporting players—P.J. Tucker, Eric Gordon, and Trevor Ariza.

Tucker scored a career-high 22 points on Wednesday night, including going 5-of-6 from three-point range. Tucker scored just a single point and struggled mightily in Game 1. In Game 2 Tucker looked like the difference maker the Rockets wanted to sign this past offseason.

Ariza also made up for a lackluster Game 1 of his own, scoring 19 points and shooting 7-of-9 from the field in Game 2. Coming off the bench, Gordon built on his strong performance in Game 1 by scoring 27 points in Game 2, including going 6-of-9 from long distance. Gordon had been struggling in the past few playoff games when it came to his three-point shooting, but on Wednesday night, he had a more typical performance.

Game 2 played out like a photographic negative of Game 1. Everything was reversed. The Rockets looked much more interested in passing and having players move without the ball while the Warriors played at a slower pace and ran more isolation plays on offense. One need not look further than the fact that the Rockets out-assisted the Warriors 23–21. (And the Warriors picked a couple of those assists in the final minutes of the game when the outcome had been determined.)

There are a lot of things that could account for this—the Warriors feeling a little too good after that Game 1 win, the Rockets getting angry after hearing people say the series was over after one game, and just some luck.

Nevertheless, the Western Conference Finals are tied up at 1–1 as things shift to Oakland for Games 3 and 4. The Warriors still look to be in control of the series, possessing the homecourt advantage and dropping Game 2 due to unusually great games from members of the Rockets' supporting cast.

"They played great tonight," Durant said. "We'll see how we respond next game." ■

The Rockets show a little razzle dazzle, as James Harden passes behind the back while being defended by Kevin Durant.

MAY 20, 2018 | OAKLAND, CALIFORNIA
WARRIORS 126, ROCKETS 85

CURRY FLURRY

Strong Third Quarter Gives Warriors Largest Win in Franchise History

After the Warriors and Houston Rockets split the first two games of the Western Conference Finals, the action shifted to Oakland for Game 3 where the Warriors looked more engaged and energized from early on they became even more dominant as the game progressed, blowing out the Rockets in the second half on their way to as 126–85 win.

The 41-point margin of victory was the largest for the Warriors franchise in the postseason while it was also the Rockets' largest postseason defeat.

This game turned in a big way during the third quarter, largely because of Stephen Curry. In the third quarter, Curry found the offensive rhythm he'd been missing in the previous two games and into the first half of Sunday night's game. In that first half, Curry had nine points and was 3-of-11 from the field, including 1-of-7 from three-point range. But in that third quarter, in which the Warriors outscored the Rockets by 10 points to push their lead from 11 to 21, Curry scored 18 of his 35 points while going 7-of-7 from the field.

When Curry started making three-pointers, you could feel the combination of relief and joy from both Curry and the Oracle crowd. Curry was playing the incendiary style of basketball we're used to seeing from him, energizing the sellout crowd in Oakland as only he can. At one point in the midst of this dominant third quarter, Curry yelled as Oracle cheered him on "This is my f--king house!"

"A lot of it was just talking to myself," Curry said. "Almost like you've got to be your biggest fan sometimes. No matter what questions I was being asked over the first two games or what the expectations was, I had the highest expectations for myself. And you've just got to find whatever you want to get going. I mean, obviously it felt good, and you want to use that energy to show your teammates that you're here, you're with them, get the crowd into it."

Although Curry's offensive explosion deserves the most praise in the Warriors' blowout victory, another reason for the win was their stellar defensive play. The Warriors' defense forced 20 Rockets turnovers on Sunday night, leading to 28 Warriors points, while also holding the Rockets to 39.5 percent from the field and 32.4 percent from three-point range.

The Warriors contested well on the Rockets' shots, forcing them into tough attempts or shot-clock violations because they couldn't get a good look. The Warriors also did a great job defending the paint, leading to the Rockets missing numerous point-blank layup attempts.

"Tonight was just all about defense and taking care of the ball," Warriors head coach Steve Kerr said. "That's it."

The Warriors defensive effort showed not only in the relatively pedestrian games for James Harden (20 points, nine assists) and Chris Paul (13 points) but in the sub-par performances of the Rockets' supporting cast. Although those players were able to get going in Game 2, they were kept in check during Game 3.

P.J. Tucker scored just six points after putting up a playoff career-high 22 points in Game 2. Eric Gordon put up just 11 points while Trevor Ariza was held to a paltry six points.

One of the defensive standouts in the Warriors' blowout victory was Kevon Looney. As the first player

Part of a second-half scoring frenzy, Stephen Curry shoots over Chris Paul during the 126–85 victory.

off of the bench, the Warriors big man stayed with quick players like Harden and Paul. Looney also did a good job around the rim, whether grabbing rebounds or contesting shots (he blocked two of them in his fifteen minutes of action).

"We're thrilled with how he's played," Kerr said

Rookie Jordan Bell also saw meaningful minutes in Game 3. Though he didn't play quite as well as Looney did, he still held his own and came up with some good plays on defense.

Kevin Durant's shot wasn't there in the first half (he went 5-for-12 from the field), but he nevertheless went into halftime with 15 points in part by getting to the free-throw line and making his four attempts. Durant finished Game 3 with 25 points on 9-for-19 shooting and six rebounds and six assists as he provided the complementary scoring to go along with Curry's electrifying output.

Both Andre Iguodala and Draymond Green played well in Game 3. Iguodala scored 10 points, all of which came in the first half. This was very important as Curry still wasn't on track offensively, and the Warriors needed all the offense they could get. Iguodala's defense was also strong in Sunday night's win as the veteran found himself frequently switched onto Harden. However, Iguodala would leave Game 3 in the fourth quarter after banging his knee against Harden's.

Green's performance was closer to his Game 1 tour de force. He brought his impressive energy on defense, defending Harden and Paul and then switching to deal with Rockets big man Clint Capela. Green was a particular force on the boards, as he finished Sunday night's game with 17 rebounds to go with his 10 points and six assists.

Even though he fell short of a triple-double, Green did all of the things around the margins, the things that are the toughest to quantify but that play an enormous role in deciding whether or not a team wins or loses a playoff game.

In their two wins in these Western Conference Finals thus far, the Warriors have looked dominant and able to exert control over the Rockets. The Warriors will look to take a commanding 3–1 series lead at home in Game 4. ∎

Nick Young celebrates after hitting a three-pointer, one of 13 the Warriors made during the 41-point rout.

MAY 22, 2018 | OAKLAND, CALIFORNIA
ROCKETS 95, WARRIORS 92

ALL TIED UP
Woeful Warriors Fourth Quarter Results in Home Loss

After their dominant Game 3 performance, the Golden State Warriors looked to claim a commanding series lead in the Western Conference Finals in Game 4—even without Andre Iguodala in the lineup. In what was easily the most exciting and closest game to date, the Warriors and Houston Rockets went back and forth, playing an exciting (if not always well-executed) game. In the end the Rockets were able to hang on by their fingernails and claim the 95–92 victory.

The Warriors started out Tuesday night's game like it was a continuation of Sunday night's blowout, opening the game with a 12–0 run while holding the Rockets scoreless for nearly five minutes. The Warriors' defense forced the Rockets into turnovers and many possessions that went deep into the shot clock in that first quarter. The Rockets had four of their 10 turnovers in the first, and those early turnovers resulted in 10 Warriors points. The Warriors also held the Rockets to 35 percent shooting from the field in the first.

It should not surprise that Draymond Green was the player leading the defensive charge. Though he faded a bit down the stretch due to fatigue (playing a remarkable 45 minutes), he scored 11 points, grabbed 13 rebounds, and handed out eight assists. But once again it was his defense that stood out, especially in the first quarter. During that early stretch, Green brought the defensive intensity that put the Rockets in an early hole.

Houston was eventually able to get their offense going and trailed by nine points at the end of the first. After struggling in the first quarter, James Harden

came alive in the second quarter. The presumptive 2018 NBA MVP scored 15 of his 30 points in the quarter to go along with Chris Paul's 14 second-quarter points. Harden's second quarter included a vicious posterization of Green.

At times in the first, it looked like Harden had checked out and wasn't up for the challenge this game presented. Starting in the second, Harden took that narrative and threw it out the window. Harden's spectacular play allowed the Rockets to come all the way back, getting the lead and pushing it to as much as 10 points before going into halftime ahead by seven.

Another reason for the Rockets' great second quarter (or the Warriors' terrible one) was a combination of Warriors turnovers and fouls. The crisp play that was on display in the Warriors' first quarter was gone as they played in a sloppy and undisciplined manner.

Five of the Warriors' 16 turnovers came in the second quarter while they also committed nine personal fouls that sent the Rockets to the free-throw line 11 times. Those extra possessions and opportunities at the free-throw line allowed the Rockets to get right back into the game.

This is where the Warriors really missed Iguodala. As has been noted so many times that has become a cliché, Iguodala is the steady presence, the one Steve Kerr referred to as "the adult in the room." That second quarter was when the Warriors could've used his steady veteran presence as they became unraveled a bit and allowed the Rockets to regain momentum.

That's what makes Iguodala so valuable and

Warriors teammates Jordan Bell and Kevon Looney try to corral the rebound during a closely contested Game 4.

important to the Warriors and why his absence is such a big one. Just how important he is to this team showed as they let the Rockets get back into a game they probably had no business being in.

After allowing the Rockets to go into halftime with the lead, the Warriors mounted another impressive third quarter that saw them regain control over Game 4. Not surprisingly, it was Stephen Curry who ignited things.

With the Warriors scuffling and the Oracle crowd considerably nervous, Curry delivered another sublime third quarter performance. Scoring 17 of his 28 points in the third, Curry dealt with a tenacious Rockets defense that pressured him and made it very difficult to get his shots off. However, Curry still managed to find the range and gave another spectacular performance before the Oracle faithful.

These Curry third-quarter explosions, which have become a common occurrence in Dub Nation, are really a sight to behold. It takes just one shot falling for the floodgates to open and the deluge to commence. The speed at which the three-pointers come crashing down upon you, the way your team's lead can turn into a double-digit deficit in the blink of an eye, it really is something that's unprecedented in the history of the NBA.

Led by Curry, the Warriors outscored the Rockets 34–17 in that third quarter as they regained the lead, possessing a 10-point advantage at the end of the third quarter. Heading into the fourth, it felt like the Warriors had weathered the Rockets' fight back and were again in control of Game 4 and poised to take the 3–1 series lead.

But much like they did in the second quarter, the Rockets showed they could withstand a powerful punch from the Warriors, using a 10–2 run early in the fourth quarter and more sloppy play by the Warriors (four fourth-quarter turnovers) to cut into their advantage.

While it was Harden who keyed the Rockets' second-quarter surge, in the fourth quarter it was Paul who really stepped up. Paul scored eight of the Rockets' 25 fourth-quarter points, coming up with important shots down the stretch that allowed the Rockets to come back and eventually reclaim the lead.

Both teams were exhausted by the time the fourth quarter began, and that showed in their play. The Warriors seemed to be especially feeling the wear and tear of this long and exhausting game, particularly with

their bench limited given Iguodala's absence. Players saw their minutes stretched beyond what they're used to. That likely accounts for the lack of ball movement (the Warriors only had one assist in the quarter) and the forced, bad shots the Warriors put up in the fourth (going 3-for-18 from the field).

"We know they're doing a lot of switching and trying to force us into one-on-one type situations," Curry said after the game. "But that's no excuse to not get the ball moving. Trusting what we do best, and whether it's the first quarter, second quarter, or crunch time in the fourth, we've got to be us, and that's going to be the adjustment for Game 5."

Kevin Durant was particularly guilty of this. Though he had a good game (27 points, 12 rebounds), Durant was 1-for-5 from the field in the fourth and took quite a few ill-advised shots. To be certain, all the Warriors looked like they were putting up questionable shots out of sheer exhaustion, but Durant's shot selection was particularly shaky.

With all that said, the Warriors had the ball after a missed Harden three-pointer down two points with seconds to go. Durant dribbled the ball up court, passed it to Klay Thompson who got trapped by the Rockets defenders, forcing him into an ugly shot with time slipping away. Thompson, who injured his knee in the second quarter but returned to the game, came up short on his shot attempt, and the Rockets secured the ball with under a second remaining, allowing them to hang on for the come-from-behind win.

The Warriors did have a timeout, and many wondered why Kerr elected to not take it. Some of that had to do with wanting to keep things spread out and flowing (Durant's winning shot in Game 3 of the 2017 Finals comes to mind). But when things got bottled up with Thompson, Kerr did want a timeout, and Green even signaled to the referees to make the call. Unfortunately, the referees didn't see Green signaling for the timeout and play wasn't stopped.

"Well, I wanted the timeout," Kerr said. "Draymond was trying to call one around four seconds. Once he got trapped, and at that point, the officials weren't looking and they're not going to look down at our bench. So I saw Draymond trying to call it, and I was hoping they'd give it to us, but we didn't get it." ∎

In a matchup of two of the best guards in the NBA, James Harden defends Stephen Curry in Game 4.

WESTERN CONFERENCE FINALS, GAME 5
MAY 24, 2018 | HOUSTON, TEXAS
ROCKETS 98, WARRIORS 94

SLOW START

Paul and Gordon Shine in Back-and-Forth Contest

After splitting the first four games of the Western Conference Finals, the Houston Rockets claimed a 3–2 series lead over the Golden State Warriors with their 98–94 Game 5 victory in Houston, putting the defending champions on the brink of elimination. It was a game that went down to the closing seconds, which was impressive given that the Warriors trailed for most of the first half—by as many as 11 points—though the game would be tied at 45 at halftime.

The Warriors' struggles from the end of Game 4 continued into the beginning of Game 5. The Warriors went 1-of-6 from three-point range in the first quarter, allowing the Rockets to get out to a big lead while the Warriors gave the ball away eight times in the first half. The Warriors were able to come back in that first half and go into halftime tied mainly because of Kevin Durant, who scored 18 of his 29 points in the first half and gave the Warriors a steady presence on offense.

Even with their struggles, the Warriors kept up with the Rockets, and it remained a close game throughout. There were 16 lead changes and 10 ties in Game 5, and all of those lead changes occurred in the second half. Klay Thompson, who scored just seven points in the first half, scored 16 in the second, including 10 in the third quarter. Stephen Curry, meanwhile, had 11 points in the first half and in the second to end Game 5 with 22 points.

But while the Warriors were able to get back into the game and held a four-point lead at one point in the fourth, they let it slip away yet again. Part of that was because Durant, who played well in the first half, struggled mightily in the game's closing quarter. Durant was 0-for-4 from the field in the fourth, taking ill-advised shots and reverting to a more isolation style of basketball.

The Rockets' play on defense, particularly that of P.J. Tucker and Trevor Ariza, was a huge factor. Throughout this series, they have played good and physical defense, making the Warriors uncomfortable and disrupting the flow of their offense.

"[T]hey're switching a lot when I get in the post now," Durant said. "I can feel them bringing a guy over, so I just got to make the right play."

For the Rockets, the offensive player most responsible for the Rockets' victory was surprisingly not James Harden, who finished Game 5 with 19 points. Rather it was the combination of Eric Gordon and Chris Paul, who were most responsible for the Rockets' win. Coming off of the bench, Gordon scored points 24 in Game 5, shedding Thompson to get open looks. Gordon has been that third offensive threat, along with Harden and Paul, and his ability to make shots are a big reason why the Rockets have been able to take the 3–2 lead in this series.

Paul, meanwhile, is seizing the moment in his

In addition to defending Klay Thompson, Rockets sixth man Eric Gordon elevated his performance in Game 5, scoring a team-high 24 points.

first trip to a conference finals. After struggling in the first half of Game 5, Paul came alive in the second. Paul scored 18 points in the second half, going 4-of-6 from three-point range. It was Paul who responded to every Warriors run and thus kept the Rockets' head proverbially above water.

On one of those three-pointers, Paul even did an impression of the famous Curry celebratory shimmy as he ran by the two-time MVP.

"It was well deserved," Curry said after the game. "It was a tough shot. If you can shimmy on somebody else, you've got to be all right getting shimmied on. So I'll keep shimmying, and maybe he will too, so we'll see what happens."

However, the closing seconds of Game 5 would dramatically alter the narrative of Paul's conference finals. After missing a floater in the lane with under a minute to go, Paul fell to the floor. After getting up Paul repeatedly grabbed his right hamstring and was unable to get back for the defensive possession. The Rockets called timeout, and Paul made his way back to the Rockets' bench unable to put any pressure on that leg.

"Well, his spirits aren't great," D'Antoni said. "He wanted to be out there and for sure he's worried and all that. That's normal. Like I said, we'll see tomorrow how it goes."

Even trailing 3–2 in the series and facing elimination for the first time since Durant joined the team, the Warriors remained poised and confident after dropping Game 5.

"We know what we're capable of," Draymond Green said. "We know we can win two games. Obviously, I think, a sense of you've been there before is always a good feeling. You know what it takes. Then with what we've put out there on the floor the last two games, it could have easily been two wins." ■

James Harden tussles with Draymond Green in Game 5, one of the Warriors' most tightly contested playoff games of the 2018 postseason.

WESTERN CONFERENCE FINALS, GAME 6
MAY 26, 2018 | OAKLAND, CALIFORNIA
WARRIORS 115, ROCKETS 86

SECOND-HALF SURGE

Klay Thompson Goes Off, Hits Four Three-Pointers in Third Quarter

The Golden State Warriors earned a 115–86 blowout win over the Houston Rockets, sending the Western Conference Finals to a decisive Game 7 despite trailing by 17 points at the end of the first quarter and by 10 points at halftime,.

For a team facing elimination, the Warriors did not play very well to start Game 6. In addition to falling behind by 17 points, they shot 22.2 percent from three-point range while the Rockets were 50 percent from long distance in the first half, allowing them to jump out to that big lead. James Harden led the way for the Rockets, scoring 22 points in that first half while getting to the free-throw line nine times (and making eight of those shots). Inserted into the starting lineup for the injured Chris Paul, Eric Gordon was also a major contributor to the Rockets' fast start. Gordon scored 16 points in the first half, including going 4-of-4 from three-point range.

While the Warriors did not look great in the first half, they put together a dominant second half, including a 33–16 third quarter that allowed them to turn a 10-point deficit into a seven-point lead.

The dominant third quarter has become a staple of the Warriors, so much so that Steve Kerr was asked about their recurrence.

"They tend to get dialed in a little more," the head coach said during his postgame press conference. "Tonight was a pretty good microcosm of our team in many ways. We have these lapses and then we have these bursts and everything in between."

Leading the way for the Warriors was Klay Thompson. Thompson scored 12 of his game-high 35 points in the third quarter, and all 12 came from three-point range. Thompson put on a performance in Game 6 that called to mind his transcendent play in Game 6 of the 2016 Western Conference Finals in Oklahoma City.

"I don't know if I was born for it, but I definitely worked my butt off to get to this point. I mean, I guess you could say I was born for it," Thompson said. "I guess everything happens for a reason. That felt good, to be honest. I just wanted to play with as much passion as I could tonight, probably sounded more vocal than I usually am. When your back's against the wall, if your shot's not falling, you can always control your passion and how hard you play. Usually when I do that, it trickles over to other aspects of my game."

It wasn't just Thompson who played well in that second half, in which the Warriors outscored the Rockets 64–25. The Warriors shot 57.5 percent from the field and 60 percent from three-point range. Stephen Curry scored 16 of his 29 points in that dominant Warriors second half.

In his postgame comments, Curry said Draymond Green's words of wisdom helped turn things around for him.

"He just told me to slow down," Curry said. "We wanted that game so bad, and the energy in the building

Jordan Bell and Klay Thompson harass James Harden, who scored 32 points but was just 10-of-24 in Golden State's blowout win.

and how we were trying to get our way back into it defensively, that affected my offensive game, and I was just rushing a little bit, not being decisive with my shots. It was a nice little pep talk to get my confidence, came out in the second half, tried to make plays."

The Warriors' defensive effort also picked up in the second half, as they held the Rockets to 29.4 percent from the field and 23.5 percent from three-point range. As the game went along, it appeared as though the Rockets had run out of energy, having used it up to jump out to that early lead in the first half. The Warriors, meanwhile, displayed the poise and confidence of a championship team, weathering the early storm and not straying from their gameplan.

"It was kind of a strange game because our defense has been really good throughout the series, and tonight it was awful to start the game," Kerr said. "We lost people in transition. We didn't communicate. We gave up wide-open threes. They scored 39 points in the first quarter. It was sort of a head scratcher…But the defense eventually kicked in, and obviously that led to transition, and the shotmaking in the second half was just amazing."

The Warriors also won the turnover battle, as they forced the Rockets into 21 turnovers while only committing 12 of their own. Between those turnovers (which resulted in 23 Warriors points) and their 13 offensive rebounds, the Warriors ended up taking 10 more field-goal attempts than the Rockets, allowing them to have more opportunities to score.

At times it looked like their season might have been over, but in the end, the Warriors rallied with a second half for the ages to force a Game 7 at Houston's Toyota Center. They'll need one more if they want to return to the NBA Finals for the fourth straight season. ■

Everyone wants a piece of Stephen Curry, who blistered the Rockets for 29 points during the Game 6 victory.

MAY 28, 2018 | HOUSTON, TEXAS
WARRIORS 101, ROCKETS 92

HOW THE WEST WAS WON

The Two Stars, Curry and Durant, Lead Second-Half Comeback

The Golden State Warriors came from behind yet again to win Game 7 of the Western Conference Finals 101–92 after trailing by as many as 15 points in the first half. With the win the Warriors won the Western Conference and advanced to the NBA Finals for the fourth straight season.

Much like in Game 6, from the outset, it was the Houston Rockets who played like the team with the championship pedigree while the Warriors looked overwhelmed by the moment. James Harden led the charge for the Rockets with 16 points in the first half while Clint Capela was able to get free around the basket and scored 14 points of his own.

The Warriors, meanwhile, turned the ball over 10 times in that first half. Between the turnovers and the Rockets' 11 offensive rebounds, the Warriors allowed the home team to take 11 more field-goal attempts in the first half. By halftime the Rockets were up by 11 points as they looked like the better team through the first half. While Kevin Durant and Klay Thompson were able to score (totaling 13 and 12 points in the first half, respectively), Stephen Curry had a sub-par first two quarters, scoring eight points on 3-of-10 shooting.

In the second half, however, things would change dramatically for both Curry and the Warriors.

It was Curry's play in the third quarter that was the most impressive. It shouldn't be that much of a surprise since Curry has been electrifying Warriors fans and the league as whole with these third quarters for many years now. Yet every time he does it, every time he takes over a third quarter and turns a substantial deficit into a sizable lead seemingly all on his own, it never fails to take our breath away.

In the third quarter of Monday night's game, Curry scored 14 of his 27 points. Curry got especially hot from three-point range in the quarter, as he went 4-of-5 from beyond the arc. Curry also had six of his nine rebounds and three of his 10 assists in that impressive third.

"You have to have endurance, you've got to have resiliency, you've got to have confidence in yourself, no matter how the game's going up until that point, that you can turn it around," Curry said of his propensity for these amazing third quarters after slow starts. "It's been great to come out of the locker room kind of focused, locked in, made some shots, get some stops, and just have fun."

Rockets head coach Mike D'Antoni brought Ryan Anderson off the bench in the third, inserting him into the lineup for P.J. Tucker. Curry went at Anderson repeatedly during that stretch, getting the forward, who is less than stellar defensively, switched onto him before putting up another three-pointer. It was vintage Curry—finding the mismatch or opening in the other team and exploiting it mercilessly.

Curry's offensive explosion would be part of a third quarter that the Warriors won 33–15, giving them a

The leading scorer of Game 7 with 34 points, Kevin Durant exploits the leaky defense of Rockets forward Ryan Anderson (33).

seven-point lead heading into the fourth. The Warriors' defense also stepped up in that third quarter, holding the Rockets to just 15 points. Curry played a large part of that, doing a good job defending Harden when the Rockets would get their All-Star guard switched onto Curry.

While Curry picked up steam as the game went on, the Rockets fizzled out. In the second half, the Rockets went a brutal 1-of-21 from three-point range. In fact they went one stretch where they missed 27 consecutive three-point shots. Both Harden and Eric Gordon cooled off considerably in the second half, forcing bad shots and reverting to a more stagnant offensive approach.

"Our talent took over," Warriors head coach Steve Kerr said of his team's second-half play. "It's as simple as that. We've got three of the best shotmakers in the league. They all got hot at different points of the second half and made great plays. We did a great job defensively too in the second half. We stayed with it."

While it was Curry's third quarter that got the Warriors the lead, it was Durant's fourth quarter that punched the Warriors' ticket to the NBA Finals. In that fourth quarter, Durant scored 11 points on 4-of-6 shooting, sealing the Warriors victory while looking like the same matchup problem he was at the beginning of this series.

"They did a great job when I get it in the post," Durant said of the Rockets' defense against him. "When I'm driving, they start to bring guys over and help and shadow a bit. I wasn't seeing that for a couple games. I was running the crowd. As I was forcing, I was going too fast on my drives and on my moves, had me just thinking too much out there."

But in Game 7 Durant shined.

"I just tried to come out and play as hard as I can on the defensive side of the ball and let my offense come around," he said, "whereas the games before I was thinking about my offense coming into the game."

That approach showed as Durant's consistency in the fourth quarter sealed the victory for the Warriors. Appropriately enough, it was the Warriors' two biggest starts—Curry and Durant—who powered the Warriors' second-half comeback. As a result, Golden State is returning to the NBA Finals for the fourth consecutive year. ∎

The Warriors pose with the Western Conference Finals hardware after reaching the NBA Finals for the fourth straight season.

The Golden State fans cheer on Kevin Durant, who has won two titles in his two years with the Warriors, after Golden State's blowout win in Game 6 of the Western Conference Finals.